Accelerated DOM Scripting with Ajax, APIs, and Libraries

Jonathan Snook
with Aaron Gustafson,
Stuart Langridge, and Dan Webb

Accelerated DOM Scripting with Ajax, APIs, and Libraries

Copyright © 2007 by Jonathan Snook, Aaron Gustafson, Stuart Langridge, and Dan Webb

ISBN-13 (pbk): 978-1-59059-764-4

ISBN-10 (pbk): 1-59059-764-8

Printed and bound in the United States of America 9 8 7 6 5 4 3 2 1

Lead Editors: Chris Mills, Matthew Moodie
Technical Reviewer: Cameron Adams
Editorial Board: Steve Anglin, Ewan Buckingham, Gary Cornell, Jonathan Gennick, Jason Gilmore,
    Jonathan Hassell, Chris Mills, Matthew Moodie, Jeffrey Pepper, Ben Renow-Clarke,
    Dominic Shakeshaft, Matt Wade, Tom Welsh
Project Manager: Richard Dal Porto
Copy Editor: Nancy Sixsmith
Assistant Production Director: Kari Brooks-Copony
Production Editor: Laura Esterman
Compositor: Linda Weidemann, Wolf Creek Press
Proofreader: April Eddy
Indexer: Beth Palmer
Artist: April Milne
Cover Designer: Kurt Krames
Manufacturing Director: Tom Debolski

Distributed to the book trade worldwide by Springer-Verlag New York, Inc., 233 Spring Street, 6th Floor, New York, NY 10013. Phone 1-800-SPRINGER, fax 201-348-4505, e-mail orders-ny@springer-sbm.com, or visit http://www.springeronline.com.

For information on translations, please contact Apress directly at 2855 Telegraph Avenue, Suite 600, Berkeley, CA 94705. Phone 510-549-5930, fax 510-549-5939, e-mail info@apress.com, or visit http://www.apress.com.

The source code for this book is available to readers at http://www.apress.com in the Source Code/ Download section.

This book is dedicated to my wife, Michelle,
for her endless support and encouragement.

Contents at a Glance

Contents

About the Authors

JONATHAN SNOOK is currently a freelance web developer based in Ottawa, Canada. A Renaissance man of the Web, he has programmed in a variety of languages, both server-side and client-side. He also does web site and web application design. Jonathan worked for more than seven years with web agencies, with clients such as Red Bull, Apple, and FedEx. He made the leap to freelancing back in January 2006. Jonathan likes to share what he knows through speaking, writing books, writing for online magazines such as Digital Web and Sitepoint, and writing for his own popular blog at http://snook.ca.

AARON GUSTAFSON founded his own web consultancy (after getting hooked on the Web in 1996 and spending several years pushing pixels and bits for the likes of IBM and Konica Minolta): Easy! Designs LLC. He is a member of the Web Standards Project (WaSP) and the Guild of Accessible Web Designers (GAWDS). He also serves as Technical Editor for A List Apart, is a contributing writer for Digital Web Magazine and MSDN, and has built a small library of writing and editing credits in the print world. Aaron has graced the stage at numerous conferences (including An Event Apart, COMDEX, SXSW, The Ajax Experience, and Web Directions) and is frequently called on to provide web standards training in both the public and private sectors. Aaron blogs at http://easy-reader.net.

STUART LANGRIDGE is a freelance hacker, published author, and noted conference speaker on DOM scripting and web technologies across Europe and the US. He's also part of LugRadio, the world's best free and open source software radio show. Aaron writes about open-source software, JavaScript, the Web, philosophy, and whatever else takes his fancy at http://kryogenix.org.

DAN WEBB is a freelance web application developer whose recent work includes developing Event Wax, a web-based event management system, and Fridaycities, a thriving community site for Londoners. He maintains several open-source projects, including Low Pro and its predecessor the Unobtrusive JavaScript Plugin for Rails, and is also a member of the Prototype core team. Dan is a JavaScript expert who has spoken at previous @media conferences, RailsConf, and The Ajax Experience and has written for A List Apart, HTML Dog, Sitepoint, and .NET magazine. He blogs regularly about Ruby, Rails, and JavaScript at his site, www.danwebb.net, and wastes all his cash on hip hop records and rare sneakers.

About the Technical Reviewer

CAMERON ADAMS (The Man in Blue) melds a background in computer science with more than eight years of experience in graphic design to create a unique approach to interface design. Using the latest technologies, he likes to play in the intersection between design and code to produce innovative but usable sites and applications. In addition to the projects he's currently tinkering with, Cameron writes about the Internet and design in general on his well-respected blog (`www.themaninblue.com`), and has written several books on topics ranging from JavaScript, to CSS, to design.

Acknowledgments

I'd like to take the time to acknowledge the many people who helped and inspired me to write this book. Thanks to the entire Apress team, especially Chris Mills and Richard Dal Porto, for being so incredibly patient. I'm also honored to have such great and knowledgeable coauthors: Dan Webb, Aaron Gustafson, and Stuart Langridge. Thanks much to Cameron Adams for doing the tech review. I'll be sure to buy you all a drink the next time we meet in person.

A big thanks to the many people within the JavaScript community who continue to share their knowledge with everybody, including Douglas Crockford, Andrew Dupont, Dustin Diaz, Dean Edwards, Christian Heilmann, Peter-Paul Koch (PPK), Stuart Colville, Joe Hewitt, John Resig, and many more I'm sure I've forgotten because I have a memory like a sieve.

Finally, this book wouldn't be possible without the support of my family. Thanks to my mom, Mel, Pat, and Trish for watching Hayden when I needed a weekend to write. Thanks to my wife, Michelle, for pushing me to get this finished and giving me the support to do it.

Jonathan Snook

Introduction

Accelerated DOM Scripting with Ajax, APIs, and Libraries will give you a better understanding of JavaScript. You can then take that new knowledge and apply it to various facets of web development such as Ajax, animation, and other DOM scripting tasks. Having this deeper understanding is an important step to improving your own code as well as accelerating your development by using popular JavaScript libraries. With the popularity of DOM scripting these days, I wrote this book to shed some additional light on current techniques and hopefully add some clarity to it all.

Who This Book Is For

This book is intended for those of you who have done some JavaScript before. You understand the syntax and have put together some basic scripts such as rollovers or pop-up windows. Having experience with server-side programming is not necessary, but is always an asset.

How This Book Is Structured

This book is intended to build on introductory knowledge of JavaScript and the document object model (DOM). From there, the book delves into common topics with DOM scripting such as working with the DOM, Ajax, and visual effects.

- **Chapter 1, "The State of JavaScript":** This chapter brings you up to speed on the state of JavaScript within the industry. It then covers how JavaScript gets evaluated with the browser and what that means to the way you code. Finally, the chapter looks at debugging your scripts, providing tools that will help you as you test your own scripts.

- **Chapter 2, "HTML, CSS, and JavaScript":** This chapter runs through some important techniques with HTML and CSS that provide a solid base on which to add JavaScript. It then covers some JavaScript basics before moving on to the DOM—how to move around and manipulate it.

- **Chapter 3, "Object-Oriented Programming":** Object-oriented programming approaches within JavaScript are explained. The chapter also looks at features of JavaScript such as closures and functional programming that make it a powerful language, especially when doing DOM scripting.

- **Chapter 4, "Libraries":** JavaScript libraries have become quite pervasive, and this chapter dissects a few of the popular libraries and shows you how they can be applied easily to your projects. The chapter also breaks down what to look for in a library.

- **Chapter 5, "Ajax and Data Exchange":** Ajax is everywhere. This chapter explains what Ajax is and what goes into an Ajax request. It describes the pitfalls of Ajax and how to plan for them. You also look at data exchange formats, learning which are most appropriate for you and when to use them.

- **Chapter 6, "Visual Effects":** Visual effects might seem superfluous, but this chapter sheds some light on the effective use of animation within your pages to enhance usability. You see how to build your own animation object and how to use JavaScript libraries to do animation.

- **Chapter 7, "Form Validation and JavaScript":** Form validation is one of the most common tasks given to JavaScript, and DOM scripting is incredibly useful when attempting it. This chapter tackles form validation on the client side with techniques such as preventing the form from being submitted, using JavaScript, and using the DOM to display error messages.

- **Chapter 8, "Case Study: FAQ Facelift":** This case study demonstrates how to show and hide elements in a page smoothly and elegantly. The application is built with progressive enhancement in mind and uses CSS, HTML, and DOM scripting to create a modern FAQ page.

- **Chapter 9, "A Dynamic Help System":** The final chapter consists of an online help system that is on hand to guide users through a suitable complicated online application. It shows how a common desktop application can be brought to the Web and provided at the touch of a button, just as it would be if it were on your desktop.

Prerequisites

The only prerequisites are a text editor to edit the scripts and a current web browser in which to test them. The code examples focus on recent browsers, including Internet Explorer 6 and 7, Firefox 2, Safari 2, and Opera 9.

Contacting the Authors

You can contact Jonathan Snook through his web site at `http://snook.ca/`.

CHAPTER 1

∎∎∎

The State of JavaScript

This chapter takes a brief walk down memory lane so you can get a sense of how the industry has changed over the last decade, including the rise of Ajax and its influence on the popularity of JavaScript. It then explains how JavaScript gets evaluated in the browser and how to plan for that. You'll learn ways to debug applications and the tools you can use to do so. It's important to understand how your code is working to fix those pesky bugs that haunt you.

JavaScript Is One of the Good Guys Again, but Why Now?

JavaScript has come a long way since its inception back in 1995. Initially used for basic image and form interactions, its uses have expanded to include all manner of user interface manipulation. Web sites are no longer static. From form validation, to animation effects, to sites that rival the flexibility and responsiveness traditionally found in desktop applications, JavaScript has come into its own as a respected language. Traditional (and expensive) desktop applications such as word processors, calendars, and e-mail are being replicated in cheaper (and often easier-to-use) Web-based versions such as Writely, 30 Boxes, and Google Mail.

Over the course of 10 years, the popularity of JavaScript has increased and waned; fortunately, it is now making its triumphant return. But why now? One word: *ubiquity* ("the state of being everywhere at once"). The goal of most developers has been to have the work they produce be available and accessible to everyone. HTML accomplished this goal early on. Much of the format matured before the Internet really took off in the late 1990s. The HTML you produced for one browser would appear mostly the same in all other browsers: Mac, PC, or Linux.

JavaScript was still quite immature, however. Its capability to interact with the HTML document was inconsistent across browsers. Its two main facilitators, Netscape and Internet Explorer (IE), implemented very different approaches, which meant that two completely different implementations were required to complete the same task. People often tried to create helper scripts, or sometimes even full-blown JavaScript libraries, to bridge the gap. Keep in mind that JavaScript libraries weren't that popular back in the day. Most saw them as bloated and unnecessary to achieve what they needed. The libraries certainly eased development, but they were large in comparison with the problems people were trying to solve with JavaScript. Remember that broadband certainly wasn't what it is today. Tack bandwidth concerns onto security concerns and entire companies disabling JavaScript outright, and you have a situation in which JavaScript seemed like a toy language. You had something that seemed the Web could do without.

With IE a clear victor of the "browser wars," Netscape languished. You might have concluded that developers would develop only for IE after it garnered more than 90 percent of the market. And many did (including me). But that ubiquity still didn't exist. Corporate environments and home users continued to use Netscape as a default browser. Clients I worked with still demanded Netscape 4 compliance, even heading into the new millennium. Building any sort of cross-browser functionality was still a hassle except for processes such as form validation.

The World Wide Web Consortium (W3C), which included partners from many of the browser developers, continued to update and finalize much of the technologies in use today, including HTML/XHTML, Cascading Style Sheets (CSS), and the document object model (DOM).

With standards in place and maturing, browser developers had a solid baseline from which to develop against. Things began to change. When Mozilla Firefox finally came out in 2004, there was finally a browser that worked across multiple operating systems and had fantastic support for the latest HTML/XHTML, CSS, and DOM standards. It even had support for nonstandard technologies such as its own native version of the `XMLHttpRequest` object (a key ingredient in enabling Ajax, which is covered in Chapter 5). Firefox quickly soared in popularity, especially among the developer crowd. The W3Schools web site, for example, shows recent Firefox usage at almost 34 percent (see `http://w3schools.com`, May, 2007).

▪**Note** Take browser statistics with a grain of salt. As the saying goes, there are lies, damned lies, and statistics. Every site is different and attracts a certain demographic, so you can expect your stats to differ from everybody else's. For example, 60 percent of those who visit my site, with its heavy skew toward developers, use Firefox. This speaks heavily to the need to build sites that work on all browsers because you never know what your users will have or how the market might shift.

Apple released Safari for the Mac, which filled the gap when Microsoft decided to discontinue developing a browser for the Mac platform. Safari, along with Firefox and Camino (based on the Gecko engine that Firefox uses), had solid support for HTML and CSS standards. Early versions of Safari had limited DOM support, but recent versions are much easier to work with and also include support for `XMLHttpRequest`. Most importantly, they all support the same set of standards.

The differences between the current versions of the browsers on the market became minimal, so you have that ubiquity you've been looking for. The reduced set of differences between browsers meant that smaller code libraries could be developed to reduce the complexity of cross-browser development. Smart programmers also took advantage of JavaScript in ways that few had done before. JavaScript's resurgence is here!

Google demonstrated that JavaScript-powered applications were ready for the mainstream. Google Maps (`http://maps.google.com/`) and Google Suggest (`www.google.com/webhp?complete=1`) were just two of many applications that showed the power, speed, and interactivity that could be achieved.

JavaScript Meets HTML with the DOM

Although this discussion is about JavaScript and its evolution, it's the DOM (which has evolved immensely from its early days) that takes center stage in the browser. Netscape, back in version 2 when JavaScript was invented, enabled you to access form and image elements. When IE version 3 was released, it mimicked how Netscape did things to compete and not have pages appear broken.

As the version 4 browsers were released, both browsers tried to expand their capabilities by enabling ways to interact with more of the page; in particular, to position and move elements around the page. Each browser approached things in different and proprietary ways, causing plenty of headaches.

The W3C developed its first DOM recommendation as a way to standardize the approach that all browsers took, making it easier for developers to create functionality that worked across all browsers—just like the HTML recommendations. The W3C DOM offered the hope of interactivity with the full HTML (and XML) documents with the capability to add and remove elements via JavaScript. The DOM Level 1 recommendation is fairly well supported across Mozilla and IE 5+.

The W3C has subsequently come out with versions 2 and 3 of the DOM recommendations, which continue to build on the functionality defined in level 1. (Differences between the DOM versions are covered in Chapter 2.)

The Rise of Ajax

The term *Ajax*, which originally stood for Asynchronous JavaScript and XML, was coined by Jesse James Garrett of Adaptive Path (`www.adaptivepath.com/publications/essays/archives/000385.php`). It was meant to encapsulate the use of a set of technologies under an umbrella term. At the heart of it is the use of the `XMLHttpRequest` object, along with DOM scripting, CSS, and XML.

`XMLHttpRequest` is a proprietary technology that Microsoft developed in 1998 for its Outlook Web Access. It is an ActiveX object that enables JavaScript to communicate with the server without a page refresh. However, it wasn't until the rise of Mozilla Firefox and its inclusion of a native version of `XMLHttpRequest` that it was used on a large scale. With applications such as Google Mail starting to take off, other browser developers quickly moved to include it. Now IE, Firefox, Opera, and Safari all support a native `XMLHttpRequest` object. With that kind of ubiquity, it was only inevitable to see the technology take off. The W3C has now moved to try and establish a standard for Ajax (see `www.w3.org/TR/XMLHttpRequest`).

Note ActiveX is a Microsoft technology that enables components within the operating system to communicate with each other. Using JavaScript with ActiveX, you can actually interact with many applications stored on the client's machine (if installed). For example, given a loose security setting, you can open Microsoft Office applications, interact with them, and even copy data out of them—all from a web page. The same can actually be done with any application that offers a component object model (COM) interface.

I mentioned XML as being one of the core tenets of Ajax, and you might wonder how XML fits into all this. As Jesse James Garrett originally describes, Ajax incorporates XML as a data interchange format, XSLT as a manipulation format, and XHTML as a presentation format. While XML was originally described as a major component of Ajax, that strict description has loosened and now describes the process of communicating with the server via JavaScript using the `XMLHttpRequest` object and the many technologies that are involved in implementing a site or an application using Ajax (such as HTML and JSON).

Ajax enables communication with the server without requiring a page refresh. But what does that mean to you? It gives you the ability to perform asynchronous actions (hence the first *A* in Ajax). You can perform form validation before the form has even been submitted. For example, have you ever tried signing up for a service only to find that the user ID was already taken? You'd hit the Back button, try a different name (and retype your password because it is never retained), and resubmit. This cycle would annoyingly repeat itself until you found an unused name. With Ajax, you can check the user ID while the user is completing the rest of the form. If the name is taken, an error message displays to the user, who can fix it before submitting the form.

With this new power, developers have been pulling out all the stops to build some dazzling applications. Alas, many are more glitz than guts; more pizzazz than power. While you might find yourself wanting to add the latest trick, it will always be important to think about usability and accessibility in all you put together. This topic will be discussed throughout the book.

Managing JavaScript

These days, JavaScript-based applications can get large and unwieldy. Before you get into any JavaScript, I want to talk about where to place code in an HTML page and the best approaches for long-term maintenance. There are some nuances that are important to remember when testing and evaluating your own code.

Code Loading

The first process to understand is the loading process. When an HTML page loads, it loads and evaluates any JavaScript that it comes across in the process. Script tags can appear in either the `<head>` or the `<body>` of the document. If there's a link to an external JavaScript file, it loads that link before continuing to evaluate the page. Embedding third-party scripts can lead to apparent slow page load times if the remote server is overburdened and can't return the file quickly enough. It's usually best to load those scripts as close to the bottom of the HTML page as possible.

```
<head>
<title>My Page</title>
<script type="text/javascript" src="myscript.js"></script>
</head>
```

Scripts that you build should appear at the head of the document and need to be loaded as soon as possible because they'll probably include functionality that the rest of the page relies on.

Code Evaluation

Code evaluation is the process by which the browser takes the code you've written and turns it into executable code. The first thing it will do is test to see whether the code is syntactically correct. If it isn't, it will fail right off the bat. If you try and run a function that has a syntax error (for example, a missing bracket somewhere), you'll likely receive an error message saying that the function is undefined.

After the browser has ensured that the code is valid, it evaluates all the variables and functions within the script block. If you have to call a function that's in another script block or in another file, be sure that it has loaded before the current script element is loaded. In the following code example, the `loadGallery` function still runs, even though the function is declared after the function call:

```
<script type="text/javascript">
loadGallery();

function loadGallery()
{
    /* gallery code */
}
</script>
```

In the following example, you'll get an error message because the first script element is evaluated and executed before the second one:

```
<script type="text/javascript">
loadGallery();
</script>

<script type="text/javascript">
function loadGallery()
{
    /* gallery code */
}
</script>
```

My general approach is to include as much of my code in functions and load them in from external files first; then I run some code to start the whole thing up.

Embedding Code Properly into an XHTML Page

Embedding JavaScript on an HTML page is easy enough, as you saw in the previous examples. Many online examples usually include HTML comment tags to hide the JavaScript from browsers that don't recognize JavaScript.

```
<script type="text/javascript">
<!--
/* run my code */
loadGallery();
//-->
</script>
```

However, the days of someone using a browser that doesn't recognize JavaScript are long gone, and HTML comments are no longer necessary.

XHTML, however, is a different beast. Because it follows the rules of XML, the script has to be enclosed into a CDATA block, which starts with `<![CDATA[` and ends with `]]>`.

```
<script type="text/javascript">
<![CDATA[
/* run my code */
loadGallery();
]]>
</script>
```

Note Throughout the book, I'll be using HTML almost exclusively; if you prefer to use XHTML, you'll need to keep this in mind.

Debugging Your Code

It doesn't matter how simple your code is, you are guaranteed to have errors in your code at some point. As a result, you'll need to have a way to understand what went wrong, why it went wrong, and how to fix it.

Alert

Probably the most common technique of JavaScript debugging is using `alert()`. There's no software to install and no complicated code to set up. Just pop a line into your code, place the information you're looking for into the alert and see what comes up:

```
alert(varname);
```

An alert is ineffective, however, for tracing anything that is time sensitive or any values within a loop. If something is time sensitive (for example, an animation), the alert throws things off because it has to wait for your feedback before continuing on. If it's a loop, you'll find yourself hitting the OK button countless times. If you accidentally create an infinite loop, you have to force the browser to close entirely, losing anything else that was open, to regain control of it—and that's never fun!

Alerts can also be ineffective because they show only string data. If you need to know what's contained within an array, you have to build a string out of the array and then pass it into the alert.

Page Logging

Page logging is a handy trick and a step above using an alert. Create an empty `<div>` on the page and use absolute positioning along with setting the overflow to scroll. Then, any time you want to track some information, just append (or prepend) the value into your `<div>`.

The script is as follows:

```
function logger(str){
    var el = document.getElementById('logger');
    // if the logger container isn't found, create it
    if(!el) {
        el = document.createElement('div');
        el.id = 'logger';
        var doc = document.getElementsByTagName('body')[0];
        doc.appendChild(el);
    }
    el.innerHTML += str + '<br>';
}
var value = 5;
logger('value = ' + value);
```

The CSS used to give the element a little style and to ensure that it doesn't interfere with the layout is as follows:

```
#logger {
    width:300px;
    height:300px;
    overflow:scroll;
    position:absolute;
    left:5px; top:5px;
}
```

Others have produced some elaborate and useful loggers that work in the same vein. Over at A List Apart, on online web magazine, there's an article on fvlogger (http://alistapart.com/articles/jslogging). Also, check out the project log4javascript at (www.timdown.co.uk/log4javascript). The log4javascript project uses a separate window to log messaging, which can be handier because it's not in the way of the current document.

Browser Plug-ins

Browser plug-ins are often beautifully crafted applications that can give you thorough minutiae on not only JavaScript but also on the HTML and CSS rendered on the page. They can be a lifesaver for learning what is actually happening on your page. On the downside, they're almost always browser-specific. That means that testing in some browsers might prove more difficult, especially if the problem is happening only in that browser.

DOM Inspector

When it comes to JavaScript development, Firefox is one of the best browsers to develop for. Its DOM support is certainly one of the best, if not the best, and it also has some of the best tools for troubleshooting. Built right in is the DOM Inspector, as seen in Figure 1-1.

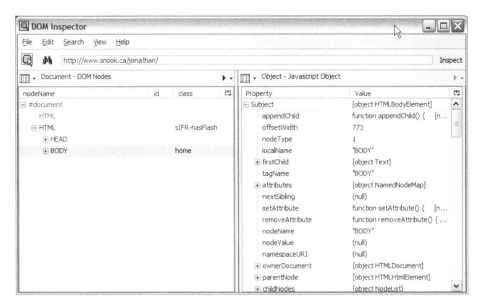

Figure 1-1. *The Firefox DOM Inspector*

With the DOM Inspector, you can navigate the document tree and view the various properties for each one. In the screenshot, you can see the properties that you can access via JavaScript. In addition, there are views for seeing which styles have been set, along with the computed values, which are handy for seeing why a layout has gone awry.

Firebug

Firebug (www.getfirebug.com) is currently the reigning champion of JavaScript and CSS debugging tools. It is by far the most powerful and flexible tool to have in your arsenal.

Firebug takes the DOM Inspector to a whole new level. Once installed, the interface panel is accessible from the status bar. The icon (see Figure 1-2) indicates whether you have any errors on the current page.

Figure 1-2. *The Firebug check mark icon*

Clicking the icon expands the interface. There's a lot of functionality packed into it, and while I won't go into everything, I do want to highlight some key features that will help in your debugging efforts.

In Figure 1-3, the Console tab is selected. JavaScript error messages, Ajax calls, Profile results, and command-line results appear in the console. Objects can be expanded to view properties, error messages can be clicked to view the offending line in the source, Ajax calls can be expanded to view request and response information, and profile results can be analyzed to discover where errors might be occurring.

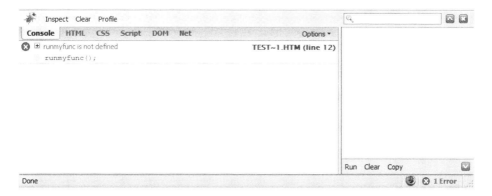

Figure 1-3. *The Firebug console*

The HTML, CSS, and Script tabs enable you to view the current state of each of those elements. You can also make changes and view them live in the Firefox window. Keep in mind that those changes are only temporary and will be lost when you refresh the page or close the window. The original files are never touched.

The DOM tab enables you to view the DOM tree and all its properties. The Net tab, as seen in Figure 1-4, shows all file requests and how long each took to load. You can use this information to determine where certain bottlenecks might be occurring.

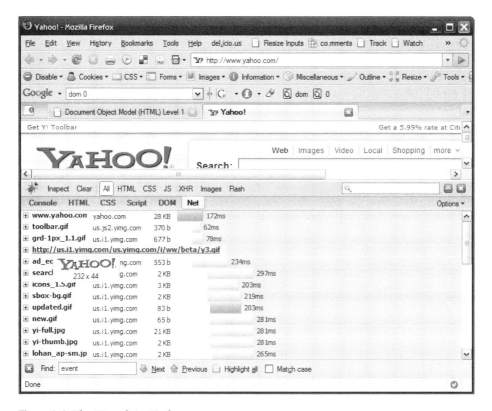

Figure 1-4. *The Net tab in Firebug*

On the main toolbar is the Inspect button, which is very useful, and you will probably use it constantly (at least, I do!). When you click the button, you can then move your mouse anywhere on the HTML page. Firebug highlights which element you are currently hovering over. It also highlights that element in the HTML tab.

With the current element selected in the HTML tab, you can see the applied style information in the panel on the right (see Figure 1-5). You can even see when certain styles have been overwritten by other styles. So as you can see, the power of Firebug extends well beyond just JavaScript.

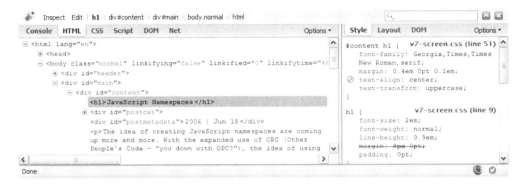

Figure 1-5. *Selected element in Firebug*

Instead of using alert statements or page logging, there are a number of hooks that Firebug adds that enable you to log information right into the Firebug console. The one I use most often is `console.log()`, which works exactly like the logger function discussed earlier, but doesn't disturb the current page—it just loads the information into the console. If you're tracing an object, you can click that object in the console and inspect all the properties of that object.

There are plenty of other features stored within Firebug, and a whole chapter could probably be written just on the gems contained within. I'll leave it up to you to discover those jewels.

HTTP Debugging

Everything you do on the Web runs over HTTP, which is the protocol that sends the packets of information back and forth.

Particularly with Ajax calls, but also useful with any server/client interaction, you'll want to see what information is actually getting sent or received. You can sometimes log this information from the back end, but that doesn't always paint a true picture of what's happening on the front end. For that, you need an HTTP debugger.

Firebug

As further evidence of its coolness, the debugger in Firebug traces Ajax calls, enabling you to view the request and the response headers, as shown in Figure 1-6. This is handy to ensure that you're receiving the correct data back. You can inspect the call to also see what data has been posted to the server and what the server returned.

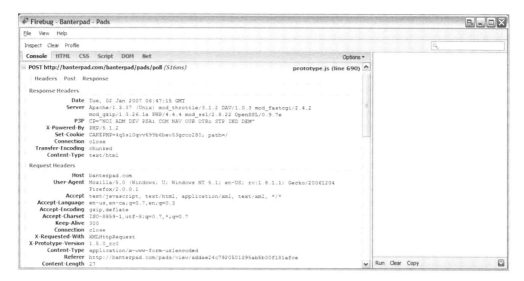

Figure 1-6. *Firebug Ajax call inspection*

Live HTTP Headers

For more fine-grained analyses of HTTP requests, I recommend that you grab Live HTTP Headers from `http://livehttpheaders.mozdev.org`. This helpful Firefox extension displays request and response info for *all* HTTP requests, which can be handy for not only Ajax calls (such as the one seen in Figure 1-7) but also monitoring page requests (including form data), redirects, and even server calls from Flash. It also enables you to replay specific requests. Before replaying data, you can even modify the headers that are being sent to test various scenarios.

Figure 1-7. *Live HTTP Headers Ajax call inspection*

Firebug reveals more response information, so you might have to bounce between it and Live HTTP Headers to get a better picture of what's going on.

ieHTTPHeaders

IE similarly has an add-in called ieHTTPHeaders to analyze the information going back and forth. It's available at `www.blunck.info/iehttpheaders.html`.

Charles

Probably the most robust HTTP debugging tool of the bunch is Charles. This debugger is shareware, so you'll have to spend a little money to include it in your toolbox—but it's money well spent for more than just tracing Ajax calls.

Charles can provide a number of useful tasks, such as bandwidth throttling for testing slow connections and spoofing DNS information for testing under a domain name before it goes live. It can automatically parse the AMF format that Adobe Flash uses for remote calls, and can parse XML and JSON used in Ajax calls. (Data exchange using XML and JSON is discussed in Chapter 5.)

The other nice thing about Charles is that it is browser-agnostic. It works as a proxy server and tracks everything through there, so you can use it with all your browsers. It's even available for Mac OS X and Linux users. (You can grab it from `www.xk72.com/charles`.)

Summary

This chapter discussed the following topics:

- Why JavaScript is becoming more popular

- How JavaScript gets evaluated in the browser

- What tools you can use to debug your code

After the quick "how-do-you-dos," you should now have a sense of why JavaScript has become the superstar it is today. You have some understanding of the things to consider when putting code into your page and have all the tools necessary to run and test the code you'll be developing from here on out. You're all set to become a JavaScript ninja!

CHAPTER 2

HTML, CSS, and JavaScript

This chapter covers HTML, Cascading Style Sheets (CSS), and how to access elements and attributes using the document object model (DOM). Discussions include event handling, creating new elements, and content styling. You learn how to leverage HTML, CSS, and DOM scripting for rapid development and easier maintenance.

Although I assume that you know your HTML and CSS, I cover some of the essentials and offer tips to make application development with DOM scripting and Ajax quicker and easier.

Getting into the Basics

You can't get any more basic than HTML when it comes to web application development. HTML is the foundation upon which all else is built, so make sure that it is solid. I won't cover what element does what because I suspect you already have a pretty good grasp of HTML if you picked up this book. What I *will* cover is a review of some of the basics that will be important going forward.

Web Standards

Although many books might discuss web standards and CSS development as the separation between content and style, using web standards appropriately can actually make application development easier, too. In old-fashioned web development—the techniques you might have learned in the 1990s, with tables and <font> tags—HTML is used as a presentation language. People would litter their code with whatever it took to make the design look as it should. This was problematic because it made site updates difficult and confusing—especially to someone who was jumping into the project for the first time.

The Web Standards Project (WaSP [see www.webstandards.org]), with people such as Jeffrey Zeldman and Molly Holzschlag at the helm, sought to provide a new approach to web development that would actually make it easier for people to develop the sites we love. There are three general facets to using web standards:

- Use CSS for presentation

- Write valid HTML

- Write semantic HTML to add meaning to the content

Of course, you might be wondering about JavaScript at this point, and you might have heard of the three-tier web development methodology of HTML for structure, CSS for style, and JavaScript for behavior (meaning dynamic functionality). It is definitely related and is an important concept to bear in mind when working through this book (and for your general web development work).

When people talk about web standards, they often discuss the separation between content (the HTML) and presentation (the CSS). Likewise, you need to ensure that the behavior (the JavaScript) is separated in much the same way. The separation enables you to add functionality to your application in a discrete way that can make your application much easier to update and can reduce overall bandwidth. This separation of JavaScript is called *unobtrusive* JavaScript. The Venn diagram seen in Figure 2-1 demonstrates that separation, with the intersection representing the sweet spot of potential experience.

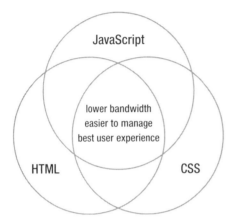

Figure 2-1. *The three elements of modern web development*

CSS for Presentation

As sites such as CSS Zen Garden (http://csszengarden.com) have demonstrated, CSS is perfectly capable of handling even the most complex design. Some approaches to using CSS effectively for web application development will be discussed later on in this chapter and throughout the book.

Valid HTML

The fault tolerance built into browsers meant that many people (including me) would rely on the way browsers displayed a particular piece of code instead of ensuring that the HTML itself was correct. Over time, as new browsers were released, differences in how browsers rendered invalid code made developing sites a hit-or-miss endeavor. Writing valid HTML helps to ensure that browsers now and in the future will render your page exactly as you intended. Valid HTML means writing to any one of the HTML or XHTML specifications set out by the World Wide Web Consortium (W3C, found at http://w3.org).

QUIRKS MODE VS. STRICT MODE

This is tangentially related to writing valid HTML. When some browsers encounter invalid HTML, they're thrown into *Quirks mode*, which is a special way to render pages and is designed to be more compatible with older browsers. However, CSS handling isn't according to specification and can make troubleshooting problems much more difficult. By writing valid HTML, browsers use a *Strict mode* that is intended to meet the W3C specifications. This results in a more reliable rendering across browsers.

If you want to test whether the HTML you have written is valid, many applications such as Adobe Dreamweaver have built-in validation tools. You can also use the W3C HTML Validation Service (see `http://validator.w3.org`).

Semantic HTML

Semantic HTML is an important and crucial point that often gets lost in the idea of creating valid HTML. Using semantic HTML means using elements that are appropriate for the content that it contains.

This is important for a few reasons. For one, those who use assistive technologies such as screen readers will have an easier time navigating your page and will also get a more natural read. Without the additional elements, the page would blur into one large block of text.

Semantic HTML also gives users more control over the page. Many designers shudder over the possibility of users messing with their finely crafted masterpieces, but trust me, it's a good thing. Designers and developers are continually making assumptions about how functional something is. It is assumed that they'll understand that something is a button or that the text is large enough. People can use user style sheets or tools (for example, Greasemonkey, a plug-in that enables users to run custom scripts on any page) to improve the readability or usability of your site or application to suit their own needs.

When it comes to web application development, using semantic HTML improves code readability, makes CSS easier to work with, and allows for additional hooks with which to tie in JavaScripting goodness.

What does semantic HTML look like? For examples, the main heading of a document should be marked up by using an `<h1>` tag, subheadings should be marked up using `<h2>` to `<h6>` tags, paragraphs should be marked up using `<p>` tags, and emphasized text should be marked up using `<em>` tags instead of `<i>` tags. If you're curious about why `<em>` tags should be used instead of `<i>` tags, just think of what italicizing is: it's presentational; there's no specific meaning to it. On the other hand, `<em>` adds emphasis. The same goes for the difference between `<strong>` and `<b>`. Simply bolding the text adds no additional meaning to it; if you want to say something strongly, use `<strong>`.

Semantic markup can also apply to your choice of class names on an element. Using `<div class="error">` is more useful than `<div class="boldRed">`, especially if you decide to change the look and feel of your error messages. This also becomes more relevant when using DOM scripting. Searching for something called `error` makes more sense than looking for something called `boldRed`.

HTML Best Practices

Although I certainly don't preach the following as gospel, I want to cover some of my personal practices and explain the reasons behind them before moving on. It's always important to understand why certain decisions are made, even if they seem to go against the popular trend. Most importantly, do what works best for you. If there's one universal truth when it comes to web development, it's that there's never just one way to accomplish something.

HTML vs. XHTML

HTML actually comes in different flavors: HTML and XHTML. XHTML 1.0 is (for the most part) just an XML-based version of HTML 4.01, the latest HTML standard. Many use and advocate the use of XHTML because it is the more recent standard available from the W3C.

XHTML certainly has a number of benefits that make it an ideal candidate for web development. Being an XML format, the document has stricter requirements about how the code itself is written. For example, all elements must be closed. To close empty elements such as images, a forward slash is placed just before the closing bracket:

```
<img src="image.gif" alt="My image" />
```

XHTML also requires that tag names be lowercase and that all attributes be quoted. Browsers that understand XHTML are stricter and tell you when you've written invalid code. Having these stricter requirements helps you produce valid code.

In XHTML, CSS and JavaScript also offer up some additional changes. In CSS, element selectors are now case sensitive. Likewise, JavaScript returns element names in lowercase instead of uppercase, as it does with HTML.

Although there are considerable benefits of XHTML, there are also some serious downsides. XHTML should be sent to the browser and identified as such by using the MIME type `application/xhtml+xml`. Unfortunately, Internet Explorer (IE) does not support this MIME type and will try to download the file or pass it off to another application to handle. XHTML 1.0 can be sent using the MIME type `text/html`, but browsers will render the page as ordinary HTML.

When serving as XML, some older DOM objects and methods—such as `innerHTML`, `document.images`, and `document.forms`—might no longer be available in some browsers.

Because of the complexities introduced by trying to develop in XHTML, I recommend developing with HTML 4.01 Strict (see `www.w3.org/TR/REC-html40`); in fact, all the examples in this book use it.

Best of Both Worlds

Just because you're using HTML doesn't mean that you can't stick to some of the better principles of XHTML. Most notably, make sure that attributes are quoted, keep your tag names lowercase, and make sure that tags are closed properly. Elements that normally close in XHTML with a closing slash don't do so when written with HTML. For example, elements such as the image (`<img>`) or the line break (`<br>`) are written without the closing slash, but elements such as list items (`<li></li>`) and paragraphs (`<p></p>`) retain the closing tag.

Maintaining XHTML-style principles keeps your code easier to read, easier to troubleshoot, and easier to transition to XHTML if and when browser support progresses to the point where it's reasonable.

CSS Basics

Like HTML, I'm assuming that you know the general CSS syntax, but I do want to review some of the basics. I will also cover some strategies to make CSS management easier, especially for interacting with JavaScript.

Say It with Meaning

Revisiting the semantic issue, I mentioned that using elements appropriate for the content is advantageous and I'll show you why in this section. Here is an example without meaning:

```
<div>This is a header</div>
<div>This is some text content.</div>
<div>Here is some additional content with <span> emphasis</span> and➥
<span>strong emphasis</span>.</div>
```

From a CSS perspective, you have no way to isolate styles to any one particular element. Obviously, it doesn't work. So, let's add some meaning:

```
<div class="header">This is a header</div>
<div class="text">This is some text content.</div>
<div class="text">Here is some additional content with <span class="emphasis">➥
emphasis</span> and <span class="strong">strong emphasis</span>.</div>
```

Look at that—the code now has meaning, doesn't it? It does, but it's terribly inefficient. You haven't taken advantage of the innate power of HTML. Let's try it one more time:

```
<h2>This is a header</h2>
<p>This is some text content.</p>
<p>Here is some additional content with <em>emphasis</em> and <strong>strong➥
emphasis</strong>.</p>
```

You accomplished two goals by using semantic HTML:

- You added meaning to the document that the browser understands. From an accessibility point of view, it also makes the document easier to understand for people who use screen readers or might have the styles disabled.

- You used less HTML, and brevity is good. The fewer bytes you have to send back and forth between the server and the client is a Good Thing™. Ajax has become popular in part because it gives you the ability to send less information (see Chapter 5). It's also one of the reasons why CSS has become popular (and why I wanted to learn it). No longer did I have to wrap `<font>` tags around everything on the page; I could use CSS to style the entire page. Better than that, the CSS file would get cached and make every subsequent page request even faster.

When you get into dealing with the CSS, you'll also discover that you can take advantage of specificity rules: something that would be made more difficult by using the same element for everything (specificity will be discussed in a bit).

Element Identifiers

HTML has two different attributes to identify an element: id and class.

An id attribute assigns a name to an element and must be unique on the page. It also has strict naming conventions that must be followed. The W3C specification says the following:

> ***ID*** and ***NAME*** *tokens must begin with a letter ([A–Za–z]) and might be followed by any number of letters, digits ([0–9]), hyphens ('-'), underscores ('_'), colons (':'), and periods ('.').*

An id attribute has several uses:

- As a style sheet selector (which has a higher specificity than other selectors)

- As a target anchor for hyperlinks

- As a means to reference a unique element using DOM scripting

The class attribute assigns a class name or multiple class names separated by a space. The same class name can be applied to multiple elements on the page. Class naming conventions are much looser than for IDs. You have letters, numbers, the hyphen, and most of the Unicode character set at your disposal. However, I recommend sticking with letters, numbers, and hyphens—anything else will be confusing.

■**Tip** Use class names that help to describe the content in a semantic way. The name "bluetext" isn't very helpful if you decide to change the design to green. Use names such as "callout" or "caption" to more accurately describe things.

As you build your application, it's important to know when to use each attribute. The quickest rule is this: if there is and will only ever be one of a particular type of element, use an id. Otherwise, you should use a class name.

Here's a quick example:

```
<div id="todolists">
    <div class="section">
        <h3>General</h3>
        <ul class="general">
            <li>Groceries</li>
            <li>Dry cleaning</li>
            <li>Buy books</li>
        </ul>
    </div>
    <div class="section">
        <h3>Programming</h3>
```

```
    <ul>
        <li>Finish project</li>
        <li>Make cool examples</li>
        <li>Write article for site</li>
    </ul>
  </div>
</div>
```

As you can see, I encapsulated all my lists in a `<div>` and gave it an ID. Each header and list is encased in a `<div>` with a section class.

Applying CSS

CSS can be specified at various levels. The three main areas are as follows:

- External style sheets (attached to the markup using the `<link>` element in the document header)

- Within the HTML document using the `<style>` element

- At the element level using the `style` attribute

Each location supersedes the previous one, meaning that declarations specified in the `style` attribute will override any declarations made previously, and any declarations specified in the `<style>` element of the document will supersede those in an external style sheet. For the most part, I recommend that you store all your declarations in one or more external style sheets. It will be easier to organize and reuse them; and when you get to DOM scripting, it will be easier to manage.

Inheritance

Inheritance, which is handy for streamlining your code, means that certain CSS properties are automatically inherited from the parent.

Using the clean HTML example from before, specifying a color for the paragraph will also mean that the emphasized text contained within it would inherit the color above it:

```
<h2>This is a header</h2>
<p>This is some text content.</p>
<p>Here is some additional content with <em> emphasis</em> and <strong>strong➥
emphasis</strong>.</p>
```

Declaring the `font-family` on the `<body>` element, for example, will be inherited by all elements on the page. You can apply different element styles, depending on which elements they are contained within. Consider the following HTML, for example:

```
<div id="main"><h2>This is a header</h2></div>
<div id="sidebar"><h2>This is a header</h2></div>
```

In the style sheet you can make the following declarations:

```
#main h2 { color:red; }
#sidebar h2 { color:blue; }
```

The header in `main` will be red, whereas the header in the `sidebar` will be blue—despite the fact that it is the same type of element being selected in each case.

Specificity

With the capability to declare styles with different types of selectors, a set of rules has been defined to determine the importance of certain declarations over others. Specificity is an important concept to grasp. As the sites or applications that you build get more complex, the selectors required to properly style an element become even more complex.

Specificity is calculated by using four levels:

A. Count 1 if the selector is the `style` attribute. Style rules take precedence over everything else.

B. Count the number of `id` attributes in the selector.

C. Count the number of other attributes (including classes and pseudoclasses) in the selector.

D. Count the number of element names (including pseudoelement names) in the selector.

Let's take a look at a few examples, each one increasing in specificity (see Table 2-1):

Table 2-1. *Specificity Examples Demonstrating Selector Weighting*

Declaration	A	B	C	D
.list {}	0	0	1	0
#todolist {}	0	1	0	0
#todolist .list {}	0	1	1	0
#todolist ul.list {}	0	1	1	1
body div#todolist ul.list {}	0	1	1	3
#pagetodo #todolist {}	0	2	0	0

There are two factors for deciding whether something has higher specificity:

- The larger number at a certain level has a higher specificity. If you had used three class selectors (level C) in a ruleset, and a second ruleset had two class selectors (also level C), the first ruleset would have higher specificity than the second.

- More importantly, a selector at a higher level has higher specificity than a number at a lower level. If you had a ruleset with an `id` selector (level B) and a second ruleset with three class selectors (level C) and an element selector (level D), the first ruleset would have higher specificity than the second.

If you find that applying a style to an element isn't working, you might think to fall back on the `!important` keyword to force the style. I recommend avoiding it if possible because it limits the amount of flexibility you have (you then have to use !important along with a ruleset with a higher specificity).

Another tip for keeping things simple is to use the fewest number of selectors possible to style an element. Then, if you are having problems with specificity, you can look to add selectors as needed.

Let's demonstrate with a quick example, starting with an HTML snippet:

```
<div id="main">
    <p class="intro">It's a fine morning today.</p>
    <p>Yes. It is a fine morning.</p>
</div>
```

Now, let's look at some CSS that could be used to style the text:

```
p { color:red; }
p.intro { color:blue; }
#main p { color:green; }
```

You might be surprised to see that the intro paragraph is green, not blue as you might have expected. The color is green because the use of the ID selector gave that declaration a higher importance over just the element selector and over the element with the class selector. Therefore, to make that intro paragraph blue as you intended, you need at least one ID selector to compete.

```
#main p.intro { color:blue; }
```

The basic rule is to figure out what level (A, B, C, or D) is forcing the specificity. Then apply a greater specificity by increasing the current level or moving up a level. If you had a ruleset with two class selectors, then you would need at least three class selectors or one ID selector. If you had one ID selector and one element selector, you'd need at least one ID selector and one class selector, or one ID selector and two element selectors, or two ID selectors.

JavaScript Basics

Although you've likely seen some of this before if you've done any JavaScript programming, I'd like to review some of the terminology and touch on some JavaScript concepts that will be important to understand before you get into the rest of the book.

Functions

Functions are a series of commands wrapped into one call. Functions enable you to encapsulate code into discrete tasks and enable you to reuse them in different ways (this will be at the core of Chapter 3 when object-oriented programming with JavaScript is covered). For example:

```
function foo(){ } // this is a function
```

Functions can also be anonymous. This means they don't have a name. They're like spirits in the wind. An example is as follows:

```
function (){ } // this is an anonymous function
```

Anonymous functions are used often in object-oriented JavaScript programming as it helps you to avoid naming conflicts and enables you to hide code that's relevant only to the object, inside the object.

Functions in JavaScript also have an added perk that you don't find in a lot of other mainstream languages: they are first-class citizens. That means functions can be assigned to variables and passed as arguments into other functions, returned from functions, and stored as an element of an array or as a property of an object.

Objects, Properties, and Methods

An object contains variables known as *properties* and functions known as *methods*. JavaScript is very powerful in that it enables you to attach new properties and methods to an object at any time, even after an object has been instantiated. Functions can actually form the structure for an object. Let's take a look at an example:

```
function foo(){ }
var bar = new foo();
```

Let's extend the last example by adding new properties to each object:

```
function foo(){ }
var bar = new foo();
foo.value = 5;
alert(foo.value); // shows the value property "5"
bar.value = 6;
alert(bar.value); // shows the value property "6"
```

Likewise, if you want to add new methods, you can do the following:

```
function foo(){ }
var bar = new foo();
foo.value = 5;
alert(foo.value); // shows the value property "5"
bar.value = 6;
alert(bar.value); // shows the value property "6"
function myfunc(){ }
bar.mymethod = myfunc; // this assigns the function
bar.mymethod(); // this calls the method
```

A variation on this is to use an anonymous function:

```
function foo(){ }
var bar = new foo();
foo.value = 5;
alert(foo.value); // shows the value property "5"
bar.value = 6;
alert(bar.value); // shows the value property "6"
bar.mymethod = function (){ }; // this assigns the function
bar.mymethod(); // this calls the method
```

In this last example, using an anonymous function means that you don't have to worry about the function `myfunc()` conflicting with any other objects or variables on the page. It also keeps the code cleaner.

■ **Note** In JavaScript, functions *are* objects. As you can see in this last example, I attached a value attribute to the foo function.

Dot Notation and Bracket Notation

JavaScript offers two ways to access the properties of an object. *Dot notation* is what I used in the previous examples. If you've done any programming in languages such as Java or C++, dot notation is very familiar. You can even chain commands together (something I do often with string manipulation).

Let's say you need to take a string that a user typed in and want to clean it up to use in the search engine:

```
// The next statement would result in "what up dog"
"What up, dog!".toLowerCase().replace(/[^a-z0-9 ]/g,"");
```

Bracket notation is similar, except properties are referenced through square brackets like an array. Using the example from the last section, you would do this:

```
alert(foo["value"]); // you should see "5"
```

You can even call methods by adding the brackets (along with any possible parameters on to the end):

```
foo["mymethod"]();
```

You can still chain items using bracket notation, too:

```
// The next statement would still result in "what up dog"
"What up, dog!"["toLowerCase"]()["replace"](/[^a-z0-9 ]/g,"");
```

This is a little harder to read, so most people stick to the dot notation. Bracket notation does give you the benefit of being able to use a variable to execute a function on an object:

```
function manipulateString(str, func)
{
   return str[func]();
}
newstring = manipulateString("WHAT UP", "toLowerCase"); // newstring = "what up"
```

In the next two chapters, you'll see some practical implementations.

Prototypes

JavaScript is prototype-based, so you essentially clone existing objects to create new objects. It also means that you can attach new properties and methods to the prototype and they'll become available for all objects, even ones that were already cloned. This is done by using the `prototype` property of an object.

Let's take the last example and build on top of it:

```
var foo = function(){ }
var bar = new foo();
foo.value = 5;
alert(foo.value); // shows the value property "5"
bar.value = 6;
alert(bar.value); // shows the value property "6"
bar.mymethod = function (){ }; // this assigns the function
bar.mymethod(); // this calls the method
foo.prototype.othervalue = 6;
alert(bar.othervalue); // shows "6"
```

As you can see, I attached the new property to the prototype of my original object foo, but it is also available under my existing object bar. (This concept is discussed in more detail in Chapter 3.)

Passing by Value or by Reference

There are two ways in which values are passed into a function: by value or by reference. When passing a variable, a copy of the value is made and used within the function. Any changes to the variable are reflected only within the function. The variable outside of the function remains untouched. This is passing by value:

```
var foo = 5;
function bar(val)
{
   val = 6; // I'm changing it to 6!
}
bar(foo);
alert(foo); // it's still 5
```

Passing an object in as a parameter will pass it in by reference. That means that you have full access to the object's methods and properties, and any changes made to the object will be reflected outside of the function.

```
var foo = function(){};
foo.prototype.value = 5;
function bar(obj)
{
   obj.value = 6; // I'm changing it to 6!
}
bar(foo);
alert(foo.value); // it's now 6!
```

Now, what happens if you try to pass in a function?

```
var foo = function(){};
foo.prototype.value = 5;
foo.prototype.addValue = function(){ foo.value = 6; }
function bar(func)
{
   func(); // I'm running the function!
}
bar(foo.addValue); // pass in the function
alert(foo.value); // it's now 6!
```

There are a couple of different things going on in this example. First, when you pass in the function, don't include the round brackets ( ) because you can pass the function in without actually executing the code contained within it. While not evident, you are actually making a copy of the function (just like the variable) and passing that in. Later on, I'll cover some things to look out for with context and object referencing.

Had you included the brackets, the function would have run immediately, and the return value of the function would have been passed through. Here's a quick demonstration:

```
function foo()
{
   return 6; // return a value
}
function bar(val)
{
   alert(val);
}
bar(foo()); // shows 6
```

JavaScript and the DOM

JavaScript is the magician that brings the HTML and CSS to life! JavaScript, the language, is pretty straightforward and I'm assuming that you've had some experience using JavaScript or at least understand the basics of the JavaScript syntax.

The power of JavaScript is in the technologies that it can use. The browser actually makes available various interfaces such as the window object, the XMLHttpRequest object, and the document object. You'll learn more about the window object and the XMLHttpRequest object in a little bit. Before that, let's talk about the DOM, which is what JavaScript uses to understand and interact with the HTML document.

What Is the DOM?

The DOM is an application programming interface (API) that defines a set of objects along with their properties and methods. The API was designed to be generic enough for both XML and HTML.

The DOM is actually a number of different recommendations, and while I refer to them as one big standard, there are actually three different recommendations with various components to each. The DOM is broken down into DOM Level 0, 1, 2, and 3:

- DOM Level 0 doesn't actually exist as a recommendation of the W3C. It is used to refer to the features available in the third versions of both IE and Netscape.

- DOM Level 1 consists of the core recommendation, which is meant for XML and HTML, and also contains an HTML-specific extension. The extension also addresses the need to be backward-compatible with the features of DOM Level 0. Many of these HTML-specific features share widespread and consistent browser support.

- DOM Level 2 adds additional XML- and HTML-specific extensions and adds support for manipulating style information, events, and ranges (handy for doing browser-based WYSIWYG editing). At this level, you start to see a divergence in how these standards are implemented across browsers.

  Mozilla browsers such as Firefox have stuck very closely to the W3C specification, whereas IE went in a different direction. For example, the current state of event handling within IE is rooted in its initial implementation that goes back beyond the point to which DOM Level 2 was even a recommendation in 1999. Unfortunately, they haven't updated the event handling since.

- DOM Level 3 adds additional extensions to the core and event handling, but most of the specification hasn't reached the recommendation level, and few browsers have implemented any of the current specification.

  Suffice it to say, you'll be sticking to Level 1 with a smidge of Level 2.

Note Although they are often referred to as *web standards*, in the academic sense they are called *recommendations*. The members of a W3C committee work together to develop a set of recommendations for all to follow.

DOM Tree Structures

The DOM is represented as a tree structure. In HTML, when a tag is inside another tag, it's considered a child element in the DOM:

```
<body>
    <div class="intro">Here is some text
        <p>More text</p>
        <p>More text</p>
    </div>
</body>
```

Figure 2-2 shows a graphical representation of how the preceding HTML looks to the DOM.

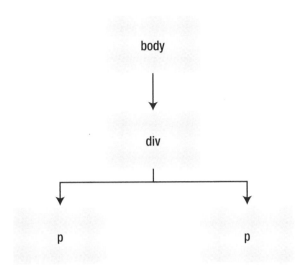

Figure 2-2. *A simple DOM tree diagram*

There are some additional subtleties to the DOM as well. For example, the DOM sees elements as node types, but an element is just one type of node. There are 12 different node types, most of which are more relevant to the XML folks. For those who work with HTML, there are only three types of nodes that are used regularly: elements, attributes, and text.

Table 2-2 shows the relevant node types.

Table 2-2. *Node Types and the Corresponding Node Type IDs*

Description	Node Type
Element	1
Attribute	2
Text	3
Comment	8
Document	9

So that last diagram is a little inaccurate because I haven't represented my attribute or text nodes. Figure 2-3 shows what the full DOM tree diagram should look like.

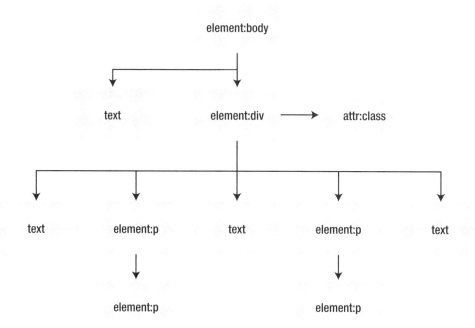

Figure 2-3. *The DOM tree diagram, with the attribute and text nodes added*

As you can see, that tree structure just got a few more branches. Keep in mind—and this is important—that even the space between tags is represented by a text node.

IE, in its usual desire to be different, doesn't recognize that blank space as a node. When you get to traversing the DOM, you'll need to keep this browser difference in mind (discussed later in this chapter).

The document Object

Now that you know what the DOM is, let's have a look at how you use it (using the document object, of course). From the document object you can reference every element on the page, add new elements, and remove existing elements.

When working with the document, there are a few functions to get one or more elements, three of which are most common:

- getElementById(): Retrieves a single element from the page.

- getElementsByTagName(): Retrieves all elements of a specific tag name. The W3C specification indicates that HTML processors generally assume uppercase elements. In current browsers, both uppercase and lowercase tag names will work. However, in XHTML, the tag name must be lowercase. Therefore, I recommend that you use lowercase.

- childNodes: A property that retrieves all nodes that are direct descendants of an element.

To see some of these functions in action, you need a document to work on:

```
<body>
    <div id="main">
        <p class="intro">Welcome to my web site</p>
        <p>We sell all the widgets you need.</p>
    </div>
    <div id="footer">
        Copyright 2006 Example Corp, Inc.
    </div>
</body>
```

Now let's play with the document a little bit:

```
var mainContent = document.getElementById("main");
mainContent.style.backgroundColor = '#FF0000';

var paragraphs = document.getElementsByTagName("p");
for(i=0;i<paragraphs.length;i++)
{
    paragraphs[i].style.fontSize = '2em';
}

var elements = document.getElementsByTagName("body")[0].childNodes;
for(i=0;i<elements.length;i++)
{
    if(elements[i].nodeType == 1 && elements[i].id) alert(elements[i].id);
}
```

First up, you grab the <div> with an ID of main and change the background color to red. Next, you grab all the paragraph elements, loop through each one, and set the font size to 2 ems. The last example grabs the <body> tag and then loops through its child nodes and pops an alert with the ID of the element.

That last example covers a few tricks. First, all elements are grabbed that have the tag name of body. Your HTML document will have only one. Therefore, you can use [0] to retrieve the first (and only) element from the collection. Next, check to see whether the node type is equal to 1. Each node type has a number. Element nodes are 1 and text nodes are 3. Attributes have a node type, but you can't retrieve them using the same methods. Instead, you use either getAttribute() to retrieve a specific attribute or attributes to access all of them.

Obtaining Elements by Class Name

As mentioned previously, one of the two ways that elements are identified is through IDs (which you can retrieve through getElementById()) and through class names. Unfortunately, there isn't a getElementsByClassName() in the specification. Since getting elements by their class name is an effective way to retrieve a set of elements, you'll make your own function to do this.

```
function getElementsByClassName(node, classname)
{
    var a = [];
    var re = new RegExp('(^| )'+classname+'( |$)');
    var els = node.getElementsByTagName("*");
    for(var i=0,j=els.length; i<j; i++)
        if(re.test(els[i].className))a.push(els[i]);
    return a;
}
```

This function takes two parameters: the node from which you want to search and the class name for which you want to search. It returns an array of elements with which you can iterate through.

Taking a look at this function, first you create a regular expression object:

```
var re = new RegExp('(^| )'+classname+'( |$)');
```

A regular expression is a syntax for doing string matching. It is very powerful, but also very confusing. I've hit my head against the wall many times trying to tame a regular expression. (See later on in this chapter for more information on regular expressions.) This particular regular expression matches a class name even if there is more than one applied to the element. The regular expression tries to find the beginning of the class name, which can either be at the beginning of the string or with a space in front of it. Then, find the class name you passed into the function. Finally, find the end of the class name by looking for a space or the end of the string. The ^ matches the beginning of a string; $ matches the end. The | is similar to JavaScript's || and checks to see whether it matches the character on the right or the character on the left of |.

Next, get all elements of the node that were passed in:

```
var els = node.getElementsByTagName("*");
```

The asterisk ("*") being passed into the getElementsByTagName() method discussed earlier means to return all elements.

Loop through the collection and test whether each class name matches the regular expression:

```
for(var i=0,j=els.length; i<j; i++)
        if(re.test(els[i].className))a.push(els[i]);
```

className is a property of an element and stores the value of the class attribute. You test that against the regular expression, which returns true if it matches. If it's true, add the current element into the array.

Finally, after you're done, pass back the array of elements:

```
return a;
```

Moving Around the DOM

After you retrieve a particular element, you often have to move around the DOM. There are four ways to do this:

childNodes: As you saw earlier, childNodes enables you to retrieve all nodes under the current element.

parentNode: Retrieves the direct parent of the current element.

nextSibling/previousSibling: Retrieves the next or previous node, respectively.

firstChild/lastChild: Retrieves the first or last child node of the current element.

Working Around Text Nodes

The way browsers handle text nodes can make moving around the DOM a little complicated. Take the following code example:

```
<div id="node">
  <p>Some text.</p>
  <p>Some more text.</p>
</div>
```

It might seem to make sense that the <div> has two childNodes; in IE, that's exactly what you get. In all the other major browsers, however, it counts the whitespace between tags as a node. As a result, you'll get five childNodes instead of just two. You'll need to take this into account when navigating from element to element by checking to see whether the node you're on is a text node or not. For example:

```
var el = document.getElementById('node');
// grab the first element
var firstElement = el.childNodes[0];
if(firstElement.nodeType != 1) firstElement = el.childNodes[1];
```

If the first element turns out not to be an element type, grab the next node. I'm making the assumption here that there is only the text node between the opening tag and the first element. Comment nodes can throw a wrench into the works. If that's the case, creating a reusable function such as the following might be advantageous:

```
function getElement(node)
{
  while(node && node.nodeType !=1)
  {
    node = node.nextSibling;
  }
  return node;
}
```

If the node passed in is an element, it skips the `while` loop altogether. Otherwise, it continues to loop until it finds a node that is an element or until it finds no more nodes (in that case, it returns `null`).

You can now rewrite the example like so:

```
var el = document.getElementById('node');
// grab the first element
var actualFirstElement = getElement(el.childNodes[0]);
```

This returns a consistent result across browsers.

■Note Whitespace in HTML includes the space, tab, line feed, form feed, and carriage return characters. Although you can't see them, each of these characters takes up space in the file. As browsers render the page, it should not render the whitespace of any text node that consists only of whitespace. Browsers also collapse multiple whitespace characters into a single space, except in `<pre>` tags. Whitespace between the opening tag and the first non-whitespace character should be ignored. Although rendering whitespace is consistent across browsers, what happens when you retrieve it via JavaScript isn't consistent. If you need consistency in all browsers when manipulating text nodes, you need to normalize the string by trimming all whitespace characters at the beginning and end of the string, along with replacing any nonspaces with spaces and then compressing multiple spaces into a single space.

Handling Attributes

You have multiple ways of handling attributes. Agnostically, you have two methods of an element that enable you to interact with attributes: `getAttribute()` and `setAttribute()`.

Suppose that the following were the HTML:

```
<a href="link.html" id="mylink">My Link</a>
```

You could retrieve the `href` attribute like this:

```
var a = document.getElementById("mylink");
var href = a.getAttribute("href");
```

Likewise, you can change the attribute using `setAttribute()` like so:

```
a.setAttribute("href", "newlink.html");
```

The HTML extensions to DOM Level 1 offer you a convenient shortcut to an element's attributes:

```
var href = a.href;
```

I prefer the brevity of this approach (you might find this to be a recurring theme with me).

In the case of the `href` attribute, there are caveats for the way different browsers behave. When using the `href` property, the full resolved URL is returned. For example, `a.href` would return `"http://example.com/link.html"`. When using the `getAttribute()` method, IE still returns the fully resolved URL, but Mozilla Firefox returns only the exact value of the attribute. For this reason, I use `a.href` for consistency.

Note There are a few differences in what the attribute property and what the `getAttribute` method return. This mostly comes back to problems with the way IE has implemented those features. For example, `getAttribute("class")` should work, but because IE simply maps the method to the `attribute` property, and because `class` is a reserved word, it doesn't work. Instead, you have to specify `className`. Tobie Langel and Andrew Dupont delve deep into the issue on Tobie's site: `http://tobielangel.com/2007/1/11/attribute-nightmare-in-ie`.

The style Property

Each element in the DOM has a `style` property that enables you to style the elements dynamically. All the CSS properties are available through the `style` property.

```
element.style.height = '100px'; // sets the height to 100 pixels
element.style.display = 'none'; // hides the element from the user
```

JavaScript doesn't like hyphens in methods or properties, so any hyphenated CSS properties have the hyphen removed and the first letter of the second word capitalized—this format is also known as camel case.

```
element.style.backgroundColor = '#FF0000'; // background is red
element.style.borderWidth = '2px'; // the border is 2px
```

You can even use shorthand CSS properties via JavaScript:

```
element.style.border = '1px solid blue';
element.style.background = 'red url(image.gif) no-repeat 0 0';
```

Animation effects can be achieved by incrementally changing an element's style properties over time (this is covered in greater detail in Chapter 6).

The class Attribute

To avoid confusion with JavaScript classes, the `class` attribute is referred to using `className`. You saw this in the `getElementsByClassName()` created earlier:

```
element.className = 'myclass';
```

Do not underestimate the power of applying a class name instead of changing style properties. Much of the Ajax interaction that you'll delve into later involves creating new elements on a page. Trying to apply multiple styles using the `style` attribute would quickly become cumbersome. Save yourself some time and define a class selector in your style sheet. Then, when the new element is added to the DOM, set the `className` attribute, and the element will be styled accordingly.

Let's go through a quick example for error handling. Here is some sample CSS that will show some red text in a rather large font:

```
.error { color:red; font-size:3em; }
```

If you detect an error in the form, you might decide to display an error message in the document instead of displaying an ugly and intrusive alert:

```
document.getElementById("frm").onsubmit = function(){
var passcode = document.getElementById("passcode");
  if(!passcode.regexp.test(passcode.value))
  {
    var el = document.createElement("div");
    el.className = 'error';
    el.innerHTML = 'Not a valid passcode';
    document.getElementsByTagName("body")[0].appendChild(el);
    return false;
  }
}
```

When it comes to rapid development, I highly recommend that you avoid applying styles directly to an element unless the value must be calculated at runtime (for example, animation).

Just as CSS establishes a separation of content and presentation with HTML, doing it in this way helps maintain a separation between presentation and behavior with JavaScript.

Inserting Content into the DOM

In the preceding example, a few more features of the DOM were used. The first is the `createElement()` method, which creates a new HTML element but sits in limbo until you insert it into the document. There are three DOM methods to add new content into the document:

- `appendChild()`: Adds the element as the last child of a parent element.

- `insertBefore()`: Adds a new element before an element that you specify.

- `replaceChild()`: Replaces an existing element in the DOM with the element that you want to add. You can also use this to replace one element with another element already on the page.

In addition to these three methods, there is a fourth (currently nonstandard) way of adding content into the document: the `innerHTML` property. This isn't part of any specification, but it has been implemented across all browsers and is even finding support in

XHTML. Firefox 1.0, for example, did not support the use of innerHTML when the document was served as XHTML. Firefox 1.1+ supports innerHTML with XHTML, though.

innerHTML enables you to specify a string of HTML that will be parsed and inserted into the document. This can be an efficient way of inserting multiple elements, attributes, or text content.

Let's do a comparison. First, use DOM methods:

```
var el = document.createElement("div");
var txt = document.createTextNode("What are you looking at?");
var img = document.createElement("img");
img.src = 'imagename.gif';
img.alt = 'I\'m wearing glasses.';
img.height = 200;
img.width = 600;
el.appendChild(txt);
el.appendChild(img);
```

Compare it with using innerHTML:

```
var el = document.createElement("div");
el.innerHTML = 'What are you looking at? <img src="imagename.gif" alt="I\'m wearing➥
glasses." height="200" width="200">';
```

Not only is it less code but it also actually performs better in the browser. However, don't accept innerHTML as a panacea. It will be important to evaluate when one approach is more appropriate than the other. Using innerHTML is great when you've got a large block of HTML that needs to be inserted; this is something you'll commonly see when using Ajax. Whereas DOM manipulation gives you some fine-grained control over inserting new elements, often a combination of techniques results in the best solution. Suffice it to say, you'll see more of innerHTML going forward.

Attaching Properties and Methods to Existing DOM Elements

Objects returned from the DOM behave just like any other JavaScript objects. This can be a handy way to store additional properties at the element level instead of in another abstracted function or object.

For example, imagine a form field that requires validation (okay, that probably wasn't very hard to imagine). You could store validation parameters at the element level.

Use the following HTML:

```
<form id="frm">
  <input id="passcode" type="text">
  <input type="submit">
</form>
```

You can then use the following JavaScript:

```
var passcode = document.getElementById("passcode");
passcode.regexp = /^[0-9]+$/;

document.getElementById("frm").onsubmit = function(){
var passcode = document.getElementById("passcode");
  if(!passcode.regexp.test(passcode.value))
  {
    alert('Not a valid passcode');
    return false;
  }
}
```

In this purely fictitious example, you grab the `passcode` element and assign a regular expression to it. Then you attach an event handler for submitting the form that can verify the contents of the field before submitting the form. If users have entered an invalid passcode, they are told, and the form is stopped from processing by returning `false`.

Browser Sniffing vs. Object Detection

One of the biggest headaches you'll run into when using JavaScript is the varying degrees to which browsers support or implement certain features. It's generally good practice to make sure, as best you can, that the browser can complete the task at hand without spitting out annoying error messages. There are a couple of ways to determine whether a browser is capable: browser sniffing and object detection.

Browser sniffing is the way it used to be done. The browser has a special object called `navigator`, within which are properties that describe the browser in some fashion or another. Most browser sniffing comes from dissecting the `userAgent` property. Here's an example:

```
" Mozilla/4.0 (compatible; MSIE 7.0; Windows NT 5.1; ➡
.NET CLR 1.1.4322; .NET CLR 2.0.50727)"
```

This is the user agent string for IE 7 on Windows XP. The problem is that browsers lie because web site developers at one point used this string to determine whether a browser was capable of using the site and would block out any user who wasn't using the "right" browser. Therefore, when browser makers were about to release a new version, they'd include a user agent string that matched closely enough to get around these issues. IE pretended to be Netscape; Opera pretended to be IE. Never mind the fact that in some browsers you can change the string to anything you want. It really was a mess.

That leaves us with *object detection*, which checks to see whether the browser supports a particular feature before it uses it. Object detection is much more reliable than string matching. You shouldn't use it to check *every* method you want to use, but at least use it to check for certain features.

For example, using `getElementById` is a good way to check that you're using a modern DOM-aware browser:

```
if(document.getElementById)
{
    var el = document.getElementById('myelement');
}
```

You can check whether the method exists by leaving off the brackets.

For a more comprehensive look at which methods are supported by which browsers, check out the support table at `www.webdevout.net/browser-support-dom`.

Regular Expressions

As discussed earlier in this chapter, regular expressions are a way to accomplish string matching (they're often referred to as regex or regexp). They are very popular, especially for validating form data, but they are tricky beasts to tame. Some of the basics are covered here, but the discussion is not exhaustive.

█Note Check out the Apress book *Regular Expression Recipes* by Nathan A. Good (ISBN: 1-59059-441-X) for a more in-depth look at regular expressions.

A regular expression can be instantiated in one of two ways. The first is by using the regular expression class:

```
var re = new RegExp('regex','ig');
```

The constructor takes two parameters, the first being the regular expression string to match and the second parameter is the flags. There are three possible flags:

i: Ignore case

g: Global match

m: Match over multiple lines

The second way to declare a regular expression is to use the literal format:

```
var re = /regex/ig;
```

The literal format does not have quotes around it; it is surrounded by the forward slash. The flags appear immediately after the regular expression.

The regular expression is meant to be used against a string. A regular expression object has two main functions: `exec` and `test`.

`exec` performs a search on a string and returns an array of matches. `test` returns `true` if a match is found and `false` otherwise. Here is a common way to test a possible American or Canadian phone number format:

```
var phonenumber = '613-555-1212';
/^\d{3}-\d{3}-\d{4}$/.test(phonenumber); // returns true
```

The `match`, `search`, and `replace` methods of the built-in `String` object accept regular expressions as parameters:

- `match` behaves like `exec` by returning an array of results that match the regular expression.

- `search` returns the index in which it could find a match within the string or returns `-1` if no match is found.

- `replace` replaces the substring match with the characters of your choosing. An example is rearranging a date format:

```
var dt = '12-01-2007';
dt.replace(/^(\d{2})-(\d{2})-(\d{4})$/, '$3$2$1'); // returns 20070112
```

A regular expression starts at the beginning of a string and works its way through trying to match to the pattern defined.

The expression can be broken down into different types of tasks. First, there's the character match itself. It might be an A or a Q or the number 8. Most often, it's a type of character or a range of characters that you're looking for. A range can be defined using square brackets with a hyphen indicating the range:

```
/[a-zA-Z]/
```

To match against any character but those in the range, just precede the range with the caret (^) character.

```
/[^a-zA-Z]/
```

You can use \w to match any letters or numbers including the underscore (\w means "word characters"), which would be the same as [a-zA-Z0-9_]. \W does the opposite and matches any character that is *not* in that range. Likewise, you can use \d just for numbers. To match any character but a newline character, use the period (.).

You can anchor the search to the beginning of the string, the end of the string, or both. To ensure that the match must start at the first character, use the caret (^) character. If it should match the last character of the string, use the dollar sign ($) character.

The following example should match any string that starts with `http` and ends in `.html`:

```
/^http.*\.html$/
```

Next there's checking for repetition of a particular character. You've already seen a couple of examples of this. For example, {2} means matching the character two times in a row. You can set up ranges such as {2,4}, which means that it must match a minimum of two characters in a row to a maximum of four characters in a row. You can leave out the second parameter to indicate that the match should start at a minimum number of characters and move up from there (example: {2,}). The + character matches the character one or more times. The * character matches the character zero or more times. In the following example, the first line makes sure that there's at least one number in a numbers-only string; the second example could match against an empty string as well as a string that has one or more numbers in it:

```
/^\d+$/
/^\d*$/
```

To remember matches, use round brackets ( ) to remember the match found. In the earlier date swap example, I'm trying to remember three separate matches. In the replace, I can refer to each of the round brackets using a $ followed by a number, which is handy for reordering the way a string might be put together.

There's obviously so much more to regular expressions than what is covered here, so I highly recommend that you take the time to learn more.

Code Formatting Practices

While there is usually never just one way to do things, it can be important to establish an approach to coding that makes it clearer for both yourself and others to understand what your code is trying to accomplish. In this chapter, I have used a particular naming convention for variables and functions.

JavaScript is commonly written using camel case. Almost all JavaScript APIs, such as the DOM and `XMLHttpRequest`, use it.

■**Note** *Camel case* is the practice of writing compound words without spaces and capitalizing each word. For example, in camel case "load calendar data" would be written as LoadCalendarData. There are two variations, upper and lower. In upper camel case, the first word is capitalized (for example, LoadCalendarData); in lower camel case, the first word is not (for example, loadCalendarData).

Variable names, function names, and object names use lower camel case, whereas classes normally use upper camel case. A class is anything that gets instantiated with the `new` keyword. (You learn all about classes and objects in Chapter 3.)

```
var element = document.createElement('div');
var object = new XMLHttpRequest();
```

Event Handling

JavaScript gets executed via an event, which might happen when the page loads, when a user clicks something, or when the document loads. Code that is not encapsulated in a function or object gets executed as soon as it is parsed by the browser. Code that is in a function or an object has to be called via an event handler.

Inline Event Handling

Similar to using the `style` attribute in CSS, you can apply an event handler to elements directly in the HTML. Let's see a click event for a link:

```
<a href="mylink.html" onclick="foo()">My Link</a>
```

When you click the link, the function `foo()` is executed. For elements that have a primary behavior, such as links or forms, the behavior runs after the event handler has completed its execution. In the previous example, after the `foo()` function is done, the user will be sent to `mylink.html`. To prevent this default action from happening, you need to return `false` as the last part of the `onclick` attribute:

```
<a href="mylink.html" onclick="foo();return false;">My Link</a>
```

Alternatively, the function can determine whether `true` or `false` should be returned and passed back to the `onclick` handler:

```
<a href="mylink.html" onclick="return foo();">My Link</a>
```

This is most commonly seen in form handlers, in which any errors in form validation return `false`, preventing the form from being submitted to the server. If no errors were found, it returns `true`, and the form is submitted to the server.

For links, you can use the `javascript:` pseudoprotocol:

```
<a href="javascript:foo()">My Link</a>
```

I definitely do not recommend that you use this practice because it's sloppy and promotes inaccessible coding practices. What do I mean by inaccessible practices? I mean inaccessible for search bots (that currently don't understand JavaScript) and inaccessible for users who have JavaScript disabled. It's best to always have a default behavior that is overridden by the event handler.

Here is an example for doing a pop-up window:

```
<a href="mylink.html" onclick="window.open(this.href);return false;">My Link</a>
```

If users have JavaScript enabled, clicking this link opens it in a new window. If users have JavaScript disabled, they can still navigate to the page.

The this Keyword

In that last bit of code, you see the `this` keyword, which enables you to refer to the current object. In this case, the `<a>` element is the current object. As you get into more advanced event handling and object-oriented programming techniques, the `this` keyword will play a prominent role.

Unobtrusive JavaScript

I previously mentioned the three pillars of separation: HTML from CSS from JavaScript. In the case of inline event handlers, you're not much better off than with style attributes. However, you can centralize all the behavior in external files and apply them to each document as required.

You do this by attaching event handlers to the objects via JavaScript. For example, if you want to run some code after the page loads, you can do this:

```
window.onload = function()
{
    foo();
    bar();
}
```

If you want to create a rollover on an image, you can do something like this:

```
image.onmouseover = function()
{
    this.src = 'newimage.gif';
}
```

Of course, you'll want to change it back when you roll out:

```
image.onmouseout = function()
{
    this.src = 'oldimage.gif';
}
```

Remember that you can store properties in an element to use them later? Let's make a more generic rollout script. You need to adjust the rollover script at the same time:

```
image.onmouseover = function()
{
    this.oldsrc = this.src; // copy the current path into a custom property
    this.src = 'newimage.gif';
}
image.onmouseout = function()
{
    this.src = this.oldsrc; // use the old path that we specified
}
```

Accessing Elements Before the Page Loads

In all the previous examples, the assumption was made that the object you were looking for existed when you asked for it. The browser makes each element on the page available via JavaScript as it reads and renders each one. However, because JavaScript code is normally included in the head of the document, the body of the document is unavailable to you. Trying to access an object before it is available will generate an error. Therefore, before you can interact with any of the elements on the page, you have to wait until the page is loaded.

As you just saw, you can wait until the page loads by using the window.onload event:

```
var el = document.getElementById("myelement"); // will generate an error message
window.onload = function()
{
    var el = document.getElementById("myelement"); // yay! I've got my element!
}
```

Oh, but there's a catch. (There had to be one.) The catch is that the onload event doesn't fire until the entire page and all its images have been downloaded. The user could be interacting with the page well before the onload event actually is run. To get around this, you have some options, but unfortunately, there's no silver bullet solution. The easiest traditional way was simply to place some JavaScript to run at the very end of the HTML page. Any HTML elements before the code should be accessible via the script. It isn't very unobtrusive, however.

The next trick is to use a timer to test for the existence of any elements before using them and then using `window.onload` as a fallback. Stuart Colville (http://muffinresearch. co.uk) did just that with his Element Ready script, which checks to see whether the element exists. If it doesn't, it checks again in a few milliseconds. It continues to check until the element is found or until the `window.onload` event fires. A personal variation on his script is shown here:

```javascript
var ElementReady={
  polled:[], /* store polled elements */
  timer:null, /* store timer */
  timerStarted: false,
  ceasePoll:function()
  {
    clearTimeout(this.timer);
    this.timerStarted = false;
  },
  startPoll:function()
  {
    if(!this.timerStarted) this.timer = ➥
setTimeout(function(){ElementReady.check(false)},100);
  },
  check:function(clean)
  {
    for(var i=0;i<this.polled.length;i++)
    {
      if(document.getElementById(this.polled[i]['element']))
      {
        this.polled[i]['callback']();
        this.polled.splice(i--,1);
      }else if(clean){
        this.polled.splice(i--,1);
      }
    }
    if(this.polled.length == 0) this.ceasePoll();
  },
  cleanUp:function()
  {
    this.check(true);
    this.ceasePoll();
  },
  chkDomId:function(elId,callback) {
      var el = document.getElementById(elId);
      if (el)
      {
        callback();
      }else{
```

```
          this.polled[this.polled.length] = ➡
{'element':elId, 'callback':callback};
          this.startPoll();
        }
    }
};

ElementReady.chkDomId('message',doStuff);
ElementReady.chkDomId('message2',doStuff2);

window.onload = function() {
  ElementReady.cleanUp();
};
```

Element Ready has a number of methods and properties, most of which are for internal use. The two key functions include chkDomId() and cleanUp(). The chkDomId() function takes two parameters: the first is the ID of the object you want to retrieve, and the second is the function you want to call once the element is available. The cleanUp() function is run on window.onload to make sure to double-check that all the elements are loaded and to run the callback function if it is.

Dean Edwards (http://dean.edwards.name) has done some testing and (with a few other folks) has come up with a way to check that the document is completely loaded that works in most browsers. Unfortunately, the solution is different for each browser, and some are only for the more recent versions of a particular browser.

```
// for Mozilla and Opera 9+ browsers
if (document.addEventListener) {
    document.addEventListener("DOMContentLoaded", init, false);
}

// for Internet Explorer (using conditional comments)
/*@cc_on @*/
/*@if (@_win32)
document.write("<script id=__ie_onload defer src=javascript:void(0)><\/script>");
var script = document.getElementById("__ie_onload");
script.onreadystatechange = function() {
    if (this.readyState == "complete") {
        init(); // call the onload handler
    }
};
/*@end @*/

// for Safari
if (/WebKit/i.test(navigator.userAgent)) { // sniff
    var _timer = setInterval(function() {
        if (/loaded|complete/.test(document.readyState)) {
```

```
            clearInterval(_timer);
            init(); // call the onload handler
        }
    }, 10);
}

// for other browsers
window.onload = init;

function init() {
    // quit if this function has already been called
    if (arguments.callee.done) return;

    // flag this function so we don't do the same thing twice
    arguments.callee.done = true;

    // do stuff
};
```

In Dean's code, the init() function is the only function that gets called. This differs from the previous approach in that instead of seeing whether the specific element you want exists and is ready for you, you instead see whether the entire document is ready for you. For the most part, you rely on the browser to tell you that it has loaded, whereas the previous script continually checked to see whether that is the case.

Attaching Events Using DOM Methods

So far, you've seen the use of attaching event handlers inline and using object properties. Inline handlers are difficult for keeping things separated, and attaching via object properties means you can attach only one handler at a time. To get around this, there is a DOM method that enables multiple event handlers to be added to a single object: addEventListener.

You might have noticed that you can add only one event handler per event. This might work well for small scripts or for large scripts in which you handle all the event handling, but (as you'll see when you get into JavaScript libraries in Chapter 4) when using other people's code that might use these events, they might not like it if you try to control everything.

The DOM offers you a solution—event listeners:

```
element.addEventListener(event, listener, false);
```

The event parameter is the event type (such as *click*, *focus* or *blur*, without the *on* prefix that you used earlier). The second parameter is the function that should execute when the event is fired (don't use the brackets because the function would fire immediately). The last parameter is a Boolean indicating whether the event handler should use capturing.

Event Capturing vs. Event Bubbling

As an event is fired, it first works its way down from the document to the element clicked (capturing) and then works its way back up (bubbling), as demonstrated in Figure 2-4. Using the

W3C approach, you can attach the event handler to either process. If you stop the event during capturing, the event won't be fired on any elements on the way down. Likewise, you can stop the event from continuing up during the bubbling phase.

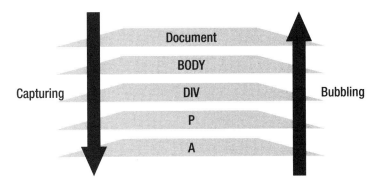

Figure 2-4. *The flow of capturing and bubbling of an event*

To stop an event from moving up and down the DOM tree, you can use the event method stopPropagation:

```
evt.stopPropagation();
```

For more information, refer to the W3C documentation at www.w3.org/TR/DOM-Level-3-Events/events.html#Events-flow. Event capturing isn't supported in IE, so it therefore tends not to be used.

Attaching Events in IE

The largest problem with events is that event handling is different in IE than the other browsers. It uses a method called attachEvent() and takes only two parameters: the event name (with *on*), and the function you want called:

```
element.attachEvent('onclick', functionname);
```

To get around this difference, you need to fork the code. You can encapsulate the event listener code into a function that you can reuse:

```
function addListener(element, event, listener) {
  if (element.addEventListener){
    element.addEventListener(event, listener, false);
  } else if (element.attachEvent){
    element.attachEvent('on'+event, listener);
  }
}
```

Now, you can add multiple event handlers to a single event:

```
addListener(window, 'load', foo);
addListener(window, 'load', bar);
```

Using event listeners are quite handy, but handling the event has become a little trickier. Remember the this keyword? When using attachEvent() in IE, the this keyword doesn't refer to the object to which you attached the event; it refers to the window object.

Let's demonstrate the problem:

```
// assume we have an a element on the page with an id of mylink
var mylink = document.getElementById("mylink");
addListener(mylink, 'click', foo);
function foo()
{
    alert(this.href);
}
```

You'd probably expect this to refer to the link, and the href would pop up, but in IE it doesn't. Let's take a moment to expand on the this keyword and see how context is handled.

Examining Context

When you run a function, the this keyword belongs to the owner of the function. The default owner is the window object:

```
function myfunction()
{
    alert(this); // this would refer to the window object.
}
```

As you add functions onto other objects, you are essentially chaining them together. One object belongs to another, which belongs to another:

```
var el = function ()
{
    alert(this); // this would refer to the window object.
}
el.methodname = function()
{
    alert(this); // this would refer to our el object
}
```

This tends to get a little confusing when you pass a method of one object as a parameter into another function:

```
var el = function ()
{
    alert(this); // this would refer to the window object.
}
el.methodname = function()
{
    alert(this);
}
```

```
function myfunc(func)
{
   func();
}
myfunc(el.methodname);
```

The path of execution bounces around, so let's step through it:

1. Create an el object and assign it a method called methodname(). If you were to run el.methodname() now, you'd get the el object.

2. Create a function called myfunc() that accepts one parameter. The function expects the parameter to be a function that it can execute.

3. Run the function passing the method of the el object in as a parameter. The myfunc() function then executes the method.

Here's where it's a little confusing. Even though you are executing el.methodname(), you passed in a reference only to the function, not to the whole object. Therefore, when you execute the function and it tries to alert this, it returns the window object because myfunc() belongs to the window object.

This can be both an advantage and a disadvantage, depending on what your needs are. Luckily, JavaScript offers a call() method that enables you to execute a method in the context of another object:

```
function myfunc(func)
{
   func.call(el);
}
```

In this example, the func function gets executed—but in the context of the el object. Therefore, when using this, it refers to el.

Many of the JavaScript libraries out there create their own methods for binding objects (this topic is discussed in more detail in Chapter 3).

Coming back to the example, you need to update the addListener() function to use call() to pass through the correct context. An anonymous function is used to encapsulate the reference:

```
function addListener(element, event, listener) {
  if (element.addEventListener){
    element.addEventListener(event, listener, false);
  } else if (element.attachEvent){
    element.attachEvent('on'+event, function(){listener.call(element)});
  }
}
```

Cancelling Behavior

Now that the events are being called, you sometimes need to cancel the event. For example, if you are doing form validation and the user has entered invalid data, you need to be able to tell the browser to stop the form from submitting.

Let's take another look at the passcode example:

```
var passcode = document.getElementById("passcode");
passcode.regexp = /^[0-9]+$/;

document.getElementById("frm").onsubmit = function(){
var passcode = document.getElementById("passcode");
  if(!passcode.regexp.test(passcode.value))
  {
    alert('Not a valid passcode');
    return false;
  }
}
```

You're not using the event listener approach here; instead, you attached the event handler directly to the element. When you attach it directly to the element, you can return `false` to cancel the default behavior of the element. In other words, if you attached an event handler to a link, you could prevent the link from being followed and (as in the passcode example) prevent the form from submitting.

When you use event listeners, you can't cancel the behavior in this way. However, the DOM event object gives you a way around this: `preventDefault()`. Let's rewrite the passcode example to use event listeners:

```
var passcode = document.getElementById("passcode");
passcode.regexp = /^[0-9]+$/;

function isPasscodeValid(evt)
{
  var passcode = document.getElementById("passcode");
  if(!passcode.regexp.test(passcode.value))
  {
    alert('Not a valid passcode');
    evt.preventDefault();
  }
}

addListener(document.getElementById("frm"), 'submit', isPasscodeValid);
```

Notice that the function is expecting a parameter. The DOM actually passes in the event object as the first parameter, which is declared as evt.

An event object stores various properties and methods about the event, such as what type of event, which mouse button was pressed (or which keys on the keyboard were pressed if it's a keyboard event), and what the target element is.

Now you have to do something different for IE. Versions older that IE version 6 don't pass in the event object as a parameter, but instead have an event object at the window level that you can access. In addition, IE's event object doesn't recognize `preventDefault();` instead, it requires use of the property `returnValue`.

Let's update the function to work in IE:

```
function isPasscodeValid(evt)
{
  evt = evt||window.event;
  var passcode = document.getElementById('passcode');
  if(!passcode.regexp.test(passcode.value))
  {
    alert('Not a valid passcode');
    if(evt.preventDefault)
    {
      evt.preventDefault();
    }else{
      evt.returnValue=false;
    }
  }
}
```

Here's a good example of the object detection described earlier. Because you don't know which browser is executing the code, you have to test for the existence of objects or methods before using them (shown in two different ways in the example). The first uses the OR (||) operator. If evt evaluates to `false` (which it will do if it's `null`, `undefined`, `0`, or `false`), assign `window.event`. The second approach tests whether the `preventDefault()` method exists. You call it without the parentheses, which will pass the function if it exists (evaluating to `true`), or as `undefined` if it doesn't (thus evaluating to `false`). You wouldn't be able to test for the existence of a property in this way if the property might actually return a value of `0`, `false`, or `null`. In that case, you'd have to be verbose and see whether the property is `undefined` using `typeof propertyName == 'undefined'`.

Tying It All Together

Let's tie all the concepts together into a single example, in which you look through all the links on the page and have all external links open up in a new window. You determine which links are external by comparing the current domain against the links on the page. If the domains don't match, it will be considered an external link.

```
function addListener(element, event, listener) {
  if (element.addEventListener){
    element.addEventListener(event, listener, false);
  } else if (element.attachEvent){
    element.attachEvent('on'+event, function(){listener.call(element)});
  }
}
```

```
function changeLinksToNewWindow()
{
    // grab the url and match up to the first "/" after the "http://"
    // grab the first (and only) match
    var currentDomain = window.location.href.match(/^http:\/\/[^\/]+/)[0];
    var elements = document.getElementsByTagName('a');
    for(var i=0;i<elements.length;i++)
    {
        // if the currentDomain is in the href, it'll return a value of 0 or more.
        if(elements[i].href.lastIndexOf(currentDomain) >= 0)
        {
            addListener(elements[i], 'click', openWin);
        }
    }
}

function openWin(evt)
{
    evt = evt||window.event;
    window.open(this.href);
    if(evt.preventDefault)
    {
        evt.preventDefault();
    }else{
        evt.returnValue=false;
    }
}

addListener(window, 'load', changeLinksToNewWindow);
```

This example is broken down into three functions and one attachment of an event handler. After the window has loaded, the changeLinksToNewWindow() function grabs all the links on the page. The function then checks to see whether the current domain name, which was retrieved from the window.location object, can be found at the beginning of each link. If they don't match, attach a click event handler so that when a person clicks the link, it opens up in a new window.

Event Delegation

Adding event handlers can at times be cumbersome, most especially when there are too many elements to attach to or when you are continually adding new elements into the DOM that have to react to events. To get around this, you can use event delegation.

Event delegation relies on an element farther up in the DOM stack to receive the event via event bubbling (see Figure 2-5). From there, you can use the target property of the event (or srcElement in IE) to determine what element was the source of the click.

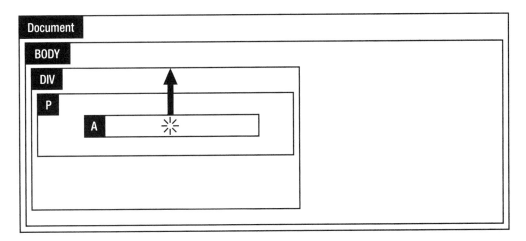

Figure 2-5. *A click event bubbling up from the link*

```
// grab the target from the event or srcElement if target doesn't exist
var target = evt.target || evt.srcElement;
```

To demonstrate event delegation, I put together this really simple match game:

```
<!DOCTYPE HTML PUBLIC "-//W3C//DTD HTML 4.01//EN" ➥
"http://www.w3.org/TR/html4/strict.dtd">
<html>
<head>
<title>Simple Match Game</title>

<link rel="stylesheet" href="site.css" type="text/css">
<style type="text/css">
li {
  padding:80px 20px;
  width:200px;
  list-style:none;
  float:left;
  border:1px solid blue;
  text-align:center;
  text-indent:-9999px;
}
li.flipped {
  text-indent:0;
}
</style>
<script type="text/javascript">
```

```javascript
var selectedPiece;
var totalMatches = 4;
var matchesFound = 0;
function checkPiece(evt)
{
  var currentPiece;
  evt = evt || window.event;
  var target = evt.target || evt.srcElement;
  currentPiece = target;

  // I clicked on a flipped piece, just ignore this move
  if(currentPiece.className == 'flipped') return;

  // show the current piece
  currentPiece.className = 'flipped';
  // if I don't have a piece already selected, use this piece
  if(!selectedPiece)
  {
    selectedPiece = currentPiece;
    return; // I've done my move
  }

  if(selectedPiece.innerHTML == currentPiece.innerHTML)
  {
    matchesFound++;
    if(matchesFound == totalMatches)
    {
      alert('You found them all! Great game!');
    }else{
      alert('good match!');
    }
  }else{
    alert('sorry, not a match!');
    // reset styles and the selected element
    currentPiece.className = '';
    selectedPiece.className = '';
  }
  selectedPiece = null; // reset selected
}

window.onload=function()
{
  var el = document.getElementById('pieces');
  el.onclick = checkPiece;
}
</script>
```

```
</head>
<body>


<ul id="pieces">
  <li>Shark</li>
  <li>Lion</li>
  <li>Lion</li>
  <li>Shark</li>
  <li>Dolphin</li>
  <li>Squirrel</li>
  <li>Dolphin</li>
  <li>Squirrel</li>
</ul>


</body>
</html>
```

In this very simple example shown in Figure 2-6, each piece is represented by a list item within an unordered list. I attached the event handler to the unordered list container (the UL).

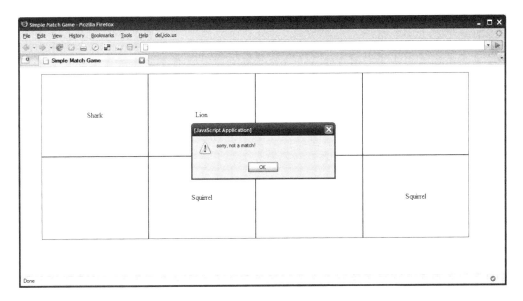

Figure 2-6. *Match game*

```
window.onload=function()
{
  var el = document.getElementById('pieces');
  el.onclick = checkPiece;
}
```

Any time something within the unordered list is clicked, the event is sent to the checkPiece function.

```
function checkPiece(evt)
{
  evt = evt || window.event;
  var target = evt.target || evt.srcElement;
  currentPiece = target;

  ...
}
```

The event target is located and assigned to a variable called currentPiece. If no piece has been selected, the current piece is assigned to a placeholder called selectedPiece. If there is a selected piece, the innerHTML is compared with that of the current piece. If they match, the user is notified and the selected piece placeholder is cleared. If they don't match, the pieces are reset and the user tries again. This continues until the user has met the total possible number of matches (totalMatches).

Halfway Between Here and There

Things get a little trickier when the element you're looking for is between the source element and the element that handled the event. Luckily, it's not all that complicated. All you have to know is how to identify the element you want, which can be through an ID, through a class name, or through a predictable HTML structure.

To get to the element that you want, start from the target and work your way back up the tree using parentNode, checking each time to see whether the element has been clicked.

Take this rather straightforward list of items, for example:

```
<ul id="test">
  <li class="theOne"><p><a href="#">To test</a></p></li>
  <li><p><a href="#">To test</a></p></li>
  <li class="theOne"><p><a href="#">To test</a></p></li>
  <li><p><a href="#">To test</a></p></li>
</ul>
```

In this case, you can see whether the user clicks any list item that has the class name of theOne. You can grab all the elements, loop through each one to determine whether it has the class name of theOne, and attach an event handler to it. Or you can use event delegation.

```
function evtHandler(evt)
{
  evt = evt || window.event;
  var currentElement = evt.target || evt.srcElement;
  var evtElement = this;
  while(currentElement && currentElement != evtElement)
  {
    if(currentElement.className == 'theOne')
```

```
    {
      alert('I have got one!');
      break; // break out of the while statement
    }
    currentElement = currentElement.parentNode;
  }
}
```

```
var el = document.getElementById('test');
el.onclick = evtHandler;
```

In this case, the event handler is attached to the entire list and acts as a catchall for anything clicked within its borders. The currentElement variable stores the event target to start off with. It's the lowest element in the stack. I check to make sure I have a valid element (I'll explain why in a second) and I check whether the current element is not the element that fired the event, evtElement. I do this because I want to check elements only from the source to the element that fired the event. I could theoretically continue up the stack until I reach the top (which I'll discover when the parentNode is equal to null, hence the check for whether the current element exists at all).

In the loop, I check to see that the current element is the one I want by matching specific criteria. In this case, I'm checking whether the class name is theOne. If it is, I perform my action and then break out of the loop (I have no reason to continue up the stack once I've found what I'm looking for). If it's not the right element, I set the current element to the parent element and start again from the top of the while loop.

Sometimes you'll know that the element you want will be a specific distance from the target element. That is, it will always be the direct parent or it will always be the sibling. In which case, you can avoid looping and just use the DOM methods to get to where you want to go.

```
target.parentNode.nextSibling.innerHTML = 'I have been found!';
```

Refer to the section "Moving Around the DOM" earlier in this chapter regarding the caveat of using nextSibling.

When Event Delegation Won't Work

There are times when event delegation isn't the most appropriate solution—usually when you have an HTML element placed over those not in the same tree structure as a result of using fixed, offset relative, or absolute positioning. Figure 2-7 shows an example of one relatively positioned element overlapping another.

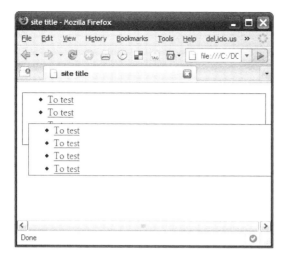

Figure 2-7. *When one element overlaps another, the overlapping element initiates the event.*

This might not seem like a common scenario—and it really isn't. Most layouts do just fine. It does, however, rear its ugly head when you drag and drop. Dragging an element over the screen, you often want the element that you're dragging over to react to demonstrate that it is a valid drop zone. However, because the dragged element is underneath the mouse cursor (using absolute positioning), you have no way to use event delegation on the document to easily pull out targets on the page.

As a result, you're left with using other means of determining whether the event is being fired over an element you want, such as offsetting the dragged element or comparing the mouse position with the position of the elements that would be drop targets.

Summary

This chapter covered a lot of ground, including the following topics:

- HTML and why semantics are important

- CSS, the importance of inheritance, specificity, and a few troubleshooting tips

- Coverage of some of the JavaScript basics

- The DOM, how to access elements and attributes, how to add new content into the DOM, and event handling

In the next chapter, you'll jump into object-oriented concepts and techniques with JavaScript. This builds on much of what you've seen here, explains some of the different techniques used so far, and goes into some more advanced JavaScript. You'll see some techniques that have really gained popularity because of many of the JavaScript frameworks that are available.

CHAPTER 3

■■■

Object-Oriented Programming

Chapter 2 covered a lot of ground, and this chapter builds on that information. I'll explain what object-oriented programming (OOP) is, and you'll learn how and why to do it with JavaScript. I'll also cover some advanced techniques for code management that can make your code more powerful and more flexible.

What Is Object-Oriented Programming?

In the last chapter, you learned what objects are in JavaScript and how to give these objects methods and properties. Object-oriented programming, often referred to as OOP, is a term that describes a number of programming concepts. Languages such as Java and C# are OOP at their core, and there's no way to avoid it. JavaScript, on the other hand, is traditionally programmed by using simple functions and variables.

If you've never done OOP before, you might ask yourself why you'd even bother. You have variables and you have functions, and if you need to reuse something, you make it a function. If you need two functions to access the same variable, you can make sure that variable is declared outside of those two functions. This process is great for small scripts, but it can turn into quite a mess of code that is hard to read and hard to maintain.

The truth is that when you use JavaScript, you're already using objects. It might be the window object, an HTML element, or an XMLHttpRequest object. In JavaScript, everything is an object. Learning to use object-oriented concepts can help you to build a more extensible application and grow beyond simple interactions. It also becomes easier for others to use your code—which is important if you want to share your code on the Internet or work in a larger team of developers.

OOP is a programming paradigm and a way of thinking when coding that can include any of the following traits:

- A *class* is the definition or blueprint for an object.

- An *object* is the result when a class is instantiated. It becomes an instance of a class. If the class is the blueprint, the object is the house.

- A *property* is like a variable in that it defines a certain state or stores a value, but is contained in an object. Properties are usually used to describe the object in some way.

- A *method* is a function that is attached to an object. A method can accept parameters, often referred to as arguments, and can return values back. Methods are used to interact with the object in some way, making it act and react. Methods are often used to change the state (that is, a property) of an object. While some languages, such as Java, require the use of methods to modify properties (also known as getter and setter methods because they get and set property values), JavaScript enables you to modify properties directly. This negates the need for overly simple methods that just change the value of a property.

- *Encapsulation* hides implementation details and restricts access to certain functionality based on what needs to access it. For example, you might have an animation object that stores a list of elements to be moved around the screen. Your code might depend on that list to be in a certain order, so you'd want to limit others from being able to access it. In other languages, encapsulation is often accomplished through private, protected, and public functions.

- *Inheritance*, which is the subclassing of objects, enables you to define subclasses that can inherit properties and methods from a parent object while offering up its own. The document object model (DOM), for example, exhibits this behavior. All elements have a generic set of methods and properties that they share, but certain elements, such as the `<select>` element, define their own methods and properties while inheriting the methods and properties from the generic element.

- *Polymorphism* allows for the same method name on two different subclasses to exhibit different behavior. For example, you might have two different Ajax subclasses: one for JSON calls and one for XML calls. Each could have a template method that takes the Ajax response and turns it into an HTML snippet. Although both inherit the Ajax communication functions from the Ajax parent class, the template methods need to act differently because of the different data formats. (If the difference between JSON and XML is lost on you, not to worry: Ajax, JSON, and XML are covered in Chapter 4.)

JavaScript, being a prototype-based language, wasn't designed to work like class-based languages such as Java or C++. However, these features can still be re-created using JavaScript's paradigm. Many developers who come from other classic OOP languages design their scripts to act and behave much like the languages they are familiar with. Having knowledge of what these OOP concepts are will strengthen your programming skills.

Now, let's get into the fun stuff.

Functions

In JavaScript, functions are at the very core of OOP because functions are objects. They provide the bare-bones structure to enable attaching methods and properties.

```
function CustomObject(){ }; // or
var CustomObject = function(){ };
```

With a function, you can use the new keyword to create new objects from your template:

```
var newObject = new CustomObject();
```

Languages that have classes have a *constructor*, which is a special method that gets executed when the new object is created and can perform some startup duties such as defining default properties or other actions.

Here's an example of a class and a constructor in Java (the important parts are bold):

```
public class Hello
{
    public static void main(String[] args) {
        System.out.println("Hello, World!");
    }
}

Hello notifyTheWorld = new Hello();
```

First, `class Hello` declares the name of the class and uses curly braces to contain all the methods within. The `main` function gets called every time you create a new object from this class. Let's look at what that code looks like in JavaScript:

```
function Hello()
{
    alert("Hello, World!");
}

var notifyTheWorld = new Hello();
```

At a quick glance, the two seem similar, yet are quite different. In Java, the `main` function is run when instantiating the new object. In JavaScript, however, instantiating the object runs the function itself. The function *is* the class definition. The code within the function gets executed each time you instantiate a new object.

This is important to know because it will affect some of the things you can do when instantiating and extending your objects.

Adding Methods and Properties

Now that you have an object, you need to give it methods and properties. I covered this in the last chapter, but let's go over it again because I'll be showing you a few different ways to do it:

```
var CustomObject = function(){ };
CustomObject.value = 5;
CustomObject.methodName = function(){ alert(this.value) };
CustomObject.methodName(); // it's 5!
```

This is great, but actually doesn't help you much because these methods and properties are accessible only on *this* object and won't be retained when you create a new object from this function (as the following example shows you):

```
var newObject = new CustomObject();
newObject.methodName(); // undefined... that didn't work.
```

To add properties to a class, use the this keyword from within the function (I'll explain why in a minute):

```
var CustomObject = function(){
   this.value = 5;
   this.methodName = function(){ alert(this.value) };
};
```

Now that your class has properties, new objects instantiated from this class will have these new properties, too:

```
var newObject = new CustomObject();
newObject.methodName(); // it's 5!
```

The properties you defined are available in any new object you instantiate.

The Mechanics of Object Instantiation

When the function is executed with the new keyword, a new object is instantiated and used as the context from within the function. Within the function, the this keyword refers to that object, and you can attach new properties and methods to that object. After your function is done, that new object is assigned to your variable.

Now you can process information before assigning it to the new object:

```
var Adder = function(valueA, valueB){
   var newvalue = valueA + valueB;
   this.value = newvalue;
   this.result = function(){ alert(this.value) };
};
var added = new Adder(5, 6);
added.result(); // it's 11!
```

Returning an Object in the Constructor

You can decide to ignore the this keyword and explicitly return your own object with methods and properties attached to it:

```
var Adder = function(valueA, valueB){
   var newvalue = valueA + valueB;
   var object = new Object();
   object.value = newvalue;
   object.result = function(){ alert(this.value) };
   return object;
};
var added = new Adder(5, 6);
added.result(); // it's 11!
```

Being able to return an object like this gives you plenty of flexibility, especially when it comes to handling inheritance. This next example uses an object literal (which will be discussed in a little bit):

```
var coreMethods = {
  add:function(a, b){
    return a + b;
  },
  minus:function(a, b){
    return a - b;
  },
  multiply:function(a, b){
    return a * b;
  },
  divide:function(a, b)
  {
    return a / b;
  }
};

var SimpleMath = function()
{
  var methods = coreMethods;
  methods.power = function(a, b)
  {
      return Math.pow(a,b);
  }
  return methods;
}


var sm = new SimpleMath();
alert(sm.power(5,6));
```

This example declared some core methods outside of the SimpleMath object. These core methods can stand alone or be applied to another object in addition to being applied to the SimpleMath object defined here.

The following shows another object that inherits the same core methods while still extending it with its own methods. It's a Pizza object that can be instantiated with the number of slices. You can then split the pizza up among friends, which automatically uses the divide method from the core methods:

```
var Pizza = function(slices)
{
  var methods = coreMethods;
  methods.split = function(friends)
  {
      return methods.divide(slices,friends);
  }
  return methods;
}

var za = new Pizza(16);
alert(za.split(4)); // alerts "4"
```

Prototype

JavaScript is called a prototype-based language (as opposed to a class-based language) because inheritance is handled through *prototype chaining*. In the previous examples, each new object that gets instantiated copies the new property and method onto each object. If you have 1,000 objects, there would be 1,000 properties and methods—each holding a special place in memory.

To avoid this overhead, there is a prototype property on which you can attach methods that are meant to be shared across all objects:

```
var Adder = function(valueA, valueB){
    var newvalue = valueA + valueB;
    this.value = newvalue;
};
Adder.prototype.result = function(){ alert(this.value) };
var added = new Adder(5, 6);
added.result(); // it's 11!
```

Only the result() method was added onto the prototype. You can't add the value property because it changes depending on the parameters that you pass into the constructor. Therefore, you have to attach that property at runtime using this.

The prototype property can also be handy because you can add properties to the base object even after you instantiate new objects. When you do so, those new properties are also available on the already instantiated objects. Let's rearrange that previous example to demonstrate:

```
var Adder = function(valueA, valueB){
    var newvalue = valueA + valueB;
    this.value = newvalue;
};
Adder.prototype.result = function(){ alert(this.value) };

var added = new Adder(5, 6);
added.result(); // it's 11

Adder.prototype.multiply = function(valueC){ alert(this.value * valueC) };
added.multiply(5); // it's 55!
```

Here's how inheritance can be handled:

```
var Dog = function(){ };
Dog.prototype.bark = function(){ alert('woof') };

var Chihuahua = function(){ };
Chihuahua.prototype = new Dog();

var sparky = new Chihuahua();
sparky.bark(); // woof!
```

There is shallow inheritance and there is deep inheritance. The example shown here is considered shallow inheritance. *Deep inheritance* means that you have a class that inherits from another class that inherits from another class, and so on. *Shallow inheritance* means that you might have a class inherit from another class, and that's it. JavaScript was never designed to allow for deep inheritance. The need for deep inheritance in JavaScript is less likely.

For more information on deep inheritance, check out the following:

- *Classical Inheritance in JavaScript,* by Douglas Crockford (`http://javascript.crockford.com/inheritance.html`)

- *Base*, by Dean Edwards (`http://dean.edwards.name/weblog/2006/03/base/`)

Object Literals

Using an *object literal* is the other primary way of creating a new object. It's also dirt simple to do:

```
var customObject = {};
```

That's it; you now have an object. Extending your object with its own properties and methods is straightforward as well:

```
var customObject = {
    customProperty: 5,
    customMethod: function(){ /* using an anonymous function*/ }
};
```

Each property contains a key-colon-value combination, and each declaration is separated by a comma. Key names get converted into strings internally. For the most part, this doesn't matter, but you can actually do some neat things if you know about it. The following is completely valid:

```
var customObject = {
    "My custom property": 5,
    5:6,
    "5":7
};
```

Keep in mind that because the keys get converted to strings, the second "5" would actually overwrite the first 5, leaving your `customObject["5"]` with a value of 7.

If you use special characters such as spaces, or if the property name starts with a number, the only way to access those properties is through bracket notation or by looping through all properties using a `for..in` loop.

You can add additional properties onto your object at any time by using dot or bracket notation:

```
customObject.value = 6;
customObject["otherValue"] = 7;
customObject.newMethod = function(){};
```

The object literal is limited in that you can't use it as a class to instantiate new objects. One object is defined, and that's it. Having only one of an object can be a very good thing. Sometimes you want only a central location to manage things (this is often referred to as a *singleton design pattern*).

■**Note** Design patterns are recurring approaches to a problem. By understanding the various approaches to solving a problem, you can choose the solution that best fits a problem you might be having. Read more about design patterns in Wikipedia at `http://en.wikipedia.org/wiki/Design_pattern_` `(computer_science)`.

The `ElementReady` object defined in the last chapter is a great example. Here's a snippet of that object:

```
var ElementReady={
  polled:[], /* store polled elements */
  timer:null, /* store timer */
  timerStarted: false,
  ceasePoll:function()
  {
    clearTimeout(this.timer);
    this.timerStarted = false;
  },
  startPoll:function()
  {
    if(!this.timerStarted) this.timer = ~CCC
setTimeout(function(){ElementReady.check(false)},100);
  }
}
```

The object literal made sense as a central point of access to control the execution of all functions with just one timer.

Keep in mind that nothing is impossible in JavaScript. If you want to create a new object from that object literal, you can use the following:

```
function object(o)
{
  function F(){}
  F.prototype = o;
  return new F();
}

var newObject = object(ElementReady);
```

The `object()` function accepts an object as an argument. It creates a new function and attaches the object to the prototype of that object, essentially copying all the properties and methods to that new object. From there, a new object is instantiated and returned. Credit for this little function goes to Douglas Crockford.

The for..in Loop

I mentioned the `for..in` loop earlier, but I want to discuss it in a little more detail because there are some things to consider when using it. If you're not familiar with the `for..in` loop, it's much like the regular `for` loop, but it enables you to loop through an object's properties, which act like an associative array:

```
// our object that we'll loop through
var coreMethods = {
  add:function(b){
    return a + b;
  },
  minus:function(b){
    return a - b;
  },
  multiply:function(b){
    return a * b;
  },
  divide:function(b){
    return a / b;
  }
};

for (var property in coreMethods) {
    alert(coreMethods[property]); // alerts each of the functions
}
```

The `for..in` loop will loop through methods and properties on the object and on the prototype. The variable before the `in` (property, in this case) gets populated with the key name. Where this can be especially tricky is if someone has extended the `Object` with custom methods. People often do this because it can be really handy. As an example, let's create an object in which you store a number of properties used to page through a set of search results:

```
var queryComponents = {
  sortBy: 'name',
  page: 1,
  pages: 10,
  resultsPerPage: 20
}
```

```
function queryBuilder(obj)
{
  var querystring = '?';
  for(var property in obj)
  {
    // make sure I have something already appended
    // before adding the & to separate values
    if(querystring.length > 1) querystring += '&';
    querystring += property + '=' + obj[property];
  }

  return querystring;
}
```

queryComponents enables you to define your query string in a convenient manner. If you want 30 results per page instead of 20, just change the value. The queryBuilder function loops through the properties of the object and builds a query string that can be passed back to the server. Running queryBuilder(queryComponents) gives you the following output:

```
?sortBy=name&page=1&pages=10&resultsPerPage=20
```

However, what happens if somebody adds to Object.prototype?

```
Object.prototype.extend = function(obj) {
  for (var property in obj) {
    this[property] = obj[property];
  }
  return this;
}
```

This function is pretty handy because it enables you to create a type of inheritance by copying the methods and properties of one object onto another. But now when you run your queryBuilder function, you get this result:

```
?sortBy=name&page=1&pages=10&resultsPerPage=20&extend=function (obj) {
    for (var property in obj) {
      this[property] = obj[property];
    }
    return this;
}
```

To check for properties that belong only to the object at hand, use the hasOwnProperty method. Here's the rewritten queryBuilder function that demonstrates it (the new addition is highlighted in bold):

```
function queryBuilder(obj)
{
  var querystring = '?';
  for(var property in obj)
  {
    if(obj.hasOwnProperty(property))
    {
      // make sure I have something already appended
      // before adding the & to separate values
      if(querystring.length > 1) querystring += '&';
      querystring += property + '=' + obj[property];
    }
  }

  return querystring;
}
```

As you loop through all the properties, check to make sure that the property belongs directly to the object and isn't from the prototype. When using a for..in loop, it's good practice to always check for hasOwnProperty.

Named Parameters

The object literal can be a handy way to handle named and optional arguments in JavaScript, as well as being able to easily define default options for an object. When you declare a function, you normally specify a number of arguments as options for that function. If anything is forgotten, it is simply passed through as undefined:

```
function func(a, b, c)
{
    alert(a); //undefined
}

func();
```

Likewise, if you care about only the first and third arguments, you still have to pass something in for the second parameter. To accept an object literal for options, the function simply accepts one parameter:

```
function func( options )
{
    alert(options.a); // alert's 5
}
var myOptions = { a: 5, b: 6, c: 7 };
func( myOptions );
```

To have default options, you can declare them within the function and then overwrite them with anything you pass into the function:

```
function func( updates )
{
  var options = { a: 5, b: 6, c: 7 };

  for (var property in updates) {
    options[property] = updates[property];
  }

  alert(options.a); // alert's 8
}
func( {a:8} );
```

The `for` loop copies all the properties in the `updates` object and attaches them to the internal `options` object.

Namespaces

Tangentially related to using object literals is the use of a namespace while developing. A *namespace* is a container for a bunch of related items. Namespaces are common and even a requirement in other languages such as Java. Although JavaScript doesn't actually have a specific construct to do namespacing, you can use the object literal and a naming convention to accomplish the same thing.

Using a namespace has a couple of benefits:

- It keeps the `global` object (also known as the `window` object) cleaner. With scripts getting larger and more complicated, along with the use of third-party scripts, there would be a much higher chance of naming collisions if everything was at the global level. Both the Prototype JavaScript library and the jQuery library use $() to retrieve HTML elements, but they behave in different ways, and the object returned will have different methods available to you. The problem is that whichever library you include last will overwrite the previous. Therefore, any code depending on the first will end up breaking. jQuery has an option that enables you to remap the $() to avoid this problem. If you think this isn't a very common situation, you'd be surprised. As of this writing, the popular site Digg.com is actually in the process of switching from Prototype to jQuery, so it has to be careful with code collisions during the transition.

- It can make your code easier to read. By encapsulating things into a single object, it establishes code ownership and enables the code within to be more self-contained. For example, any of the code on my site is in a `SNOOK` namespace, making it clear that everything is related. Likewise, the Yahoo! User Interface library (which will be covered in Chapter 4) uses `YAHOO` as its namespace. There's no confusion. In addition, I can store shared variables within the namespace that all functions within can have access to without worrying about conflicting with other scripts.

But is using namespaces necessary? Certainly not. People have lived without namespaces for the past ten years of JavaScript development. However, it doesn't hurt to keep things clean and organized from the beginning.

Here is some code from my site to demonstrate how I declared a namespace. In my blog I have a comment form that enables people to leave feedback about a particular post. When users enter their name, e-mail address, and URL, they are remembered the next time they visit the site. Once the namespace is declared, each of the methods gets attached to that object.

```
// declare the namespace
var SNOOK = {};

SNOOK.prepareCommentForm = function(){ /* initializes fields */ }
SNOOK.prepareField = function(options) { /* attaches event handlers, etc. */ }
SNOOK.setCookie = function(name, value, expires){ /* sets a cookie */ }
SNOOK.getCookie = function(name){ /* retrieves the value of a cookie */ }
SNOOK.remember = function(fld){ /* remembers the user-entered data*/ }
```

Closures

One of the vastly misunderstood features of JavaScript is its use of closures. With a *closure*, a child function has access to the environment of the parent function, even after the parent function has completed execution. In Figure 3-1, functions A and B have access to the variables and functions declared within the window object. Likewise, if functions C and D are declared within function B, they have access to all the variables and functions declared within the window object and also those within function B. Any functions declared within function C have access to all variables and functions all the way up the tree.

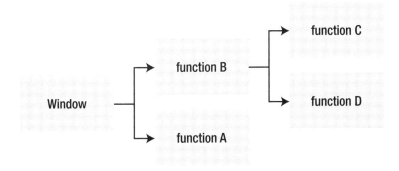

Figure 3-1. *How closures create a hierarchy of variable and function access*

The most common example of closures involves declaring event handlers:

```
function attachBehavior(){
    var element = document.getElementById('main');
    element.onclick = function(){ element.innerHTML = 'Surprise!'; };
}
```

The function that you attach to the onclick event creates a closure, so it still has access to the element variable.

As functions get passed around, they always retain access to this initial scoping. The function can be returned or set as a parameter to another function, and it still has access to its original scope. It's important to remember, though, that the function has to be declared from within the function whose variables that you want to retain access to.

```
function onclickHandler(){
    element.innerHTML = 'Surprise!';
}
function attachBehavior(){
    var element = document.getElementById('main');
    element.onclick = onclickHandler;
}
```

If you run the attachBehavior function and click your main element, you'll get an error about the element being undefined because the function was declared outside of the attachBehavior function. Even though it's being assigned to a variable from within the function, where the function gets declared is what matters.

Closures can be useful for referencing information across the divide of event handling, instead of having to worry about retaining proper access to this:

```
function launcher(element, message)
{
    function openWin()
    {
        alert(message);
    }
    addListener(element, 'click', openWin);
}

launcher( document.getElementById('mylink'),
'This link will open in a new window!' );
```

Using the addListener() function from the previous chapter, the openWin() function was attached as the event handler. However, because of the closure, openWin() still has access to the message argument after the event has been fired.

Once you get comfortable with closures, you might find yourself avoiding the use of this more often.

Closures have a bit of a stigma because of the way Internet Explorer (IE) handles them in conjunction with working with DOM objects. IE has traditionally had trouble releasing the memory when a closure is used in this way, even after navigating away from the current page. It requires the browser to be restarted to regain this memory. Microsoft resolved this problem in IE 7; it then released a patch in June 2007 for IE 6 that resolved memory leaks in that browser. Unfortunately, the patch applied only to those running IE 6 on Windows XP. Older machines or those that don't have the patch installed still have memory issues.

You might not notice the memory leak in a small application, and it would require a lot of executions to see a large impact on system performance. When you get into larger applications, though, users tend to spend more time on a single page that does a lot more DOM manipulation and event handling. The likelihood is therefore much higher that it can have an impact on your customers—especially these days, when people are less and less likely to close down their browsers on a regular basis. (I sometimes go days, if not weeks, at a time before closing my browser down.)

To avoid memory leaks, you can avoid using closures:

```
function attachBehavior(){
    var element = document.getElementById('main');
    element.onclick = onclickHandler;
}

function onclickHandler(){
    // the this keyword refers to the element clicked
    // and not our variable 'element'
    this.innerHTML = 'Surprise!';
}
```

Many of the JavaScript libraries, especially the ones covered in this book, implement their scripts to minimize the potential for memory leaks.

Encapsulation

Encapsulation enables you to hide implementation details from those who use your scripts. Remember the Java code from the beginning of the chapter?

```
public class Hello
{
    public static void main(String[] args) {
        System.out.println("Hello, World!");
    }
}
```

I highlighted in bold how Java enables a developer to show or hide implementation details from those who use the code. Public methods are an interaction point into the object. If it were set to private, only the class itself could access those functions. Likewise, if the class is set to private, only other classes in the namespace could access the class.

When developing code for other people to use, such as within a development team or as a helper script released to the public, you normally have an application programming interface (API). There are specific properties and methods that people can use; the rest just make your life easier from within the script.

Let's look at the ElementReady script:

```
var ElementReady={
  polled:[], /* store polled elements */
  timer:null, /* store timer */
  timerStarted: false,
```

```
    ceasePoll:function(){...},
    startPoll:function(){...},
    check:function(clean){...},
    cleanUp:function(){...},
    chkDomId:function(elId,callback) {...}
};
```

In this object that you're using to handle all your tasks, most of these properties are actually for internal use only. chkDomId(), cleanUp(), and check() are the only methods that are ever used from outside the object. If that's the case, should the other properties actually be accessible? Based on what you have learned about object creation and closures, you can actually redesign this class so that only those three functions are accessible. Everything else will be accessible from only those functions:

```
var ElementReady= new function(){
    var polled = []; /* store polled elements */
    var timer = null; /* store timer */
    var timerStarted = false;
    var ceasePoll = function(){...};
    var startPoll = function(){...};
    return {
        check:function(clean){...},
        cleanUp:function(){...},
        chkDomId:function(elId,callback) {...}
    }
};
```

Let me explain what was updated. The first thing I did was change the main ElementReady object from an object literal to an anonymous function that is instantiated into a new object. Now that it's no longer an object literal, the items within it are set up just like regular variables. These will be your internal or private variables. Finally, I take the three functions that I want to be available publicly and return them in an object literal.

With closures, those public functions still have access to the internal variables. The other thing that had to change was how I referred to those internal variables—I dropped the this keyword from them.

In the future, you can create a new version of the ElementReady script, and as long as the interface for those three functions hasn't changed, it doesn't matter what you've done with the rest of the implementation.

Here's the final version with the changes implemented:

```
var ElementReady= new function(){
    var polled = []; /* store polled elements */
    var timer = null; /* store timer */
    var timerStarted = false;
```

```
  var ceasePoll = function()
  {
    clearTimeout(timer);
    timerStarted = false;
  };
  var startPoll = function()
  {
    if(!timerStarted) {
      timer = setTimeout( function(){ElementReady.check(false)}, 100);
    }
  };

  return {
      check:function(clean)
      {
        for(var i=0;i<polled.length;i++)
        {
          if(document.getElementById(polled[i]['element']))
          {
            polled[i]['callback']();
            polled.splice(i--,1);
          }else if(clean){
            polled.splice(i--,1);
          }
        }
        if(polled.length == 0) ceasePoll();
      },
      cleanUp:function()
      {
         check(true);
         ceasePoll();
      },
      chkDomId:function(elId,callback) {
          var el = document.getElementById(elId);
          if (el)
          {
            callback();
          }else{
            polled[polled.length] = {'element':elId, 'callback':callback};
            startPoll();
          }
      }
  }
};
```

This type of encapsulation can also be used to create a class to instantiate a number of objects in which each object needs access to these hidden properties and methods (called *private members*):

```
function CurrentAnswer(num)
{
  var current = num;

  var newObject = {
    getCurrent: function(){ return 'The current answer is: ' + current; }
  }
  return newObject;
}

var curr = new CurrentAnswer('5');

alert(curr.getCurrent()); // alert's the string 'The current answer is: 5'
```

Like the previous example, you can define a solid API with which to interact with your object and obscure away the inner workings.

Functional Programming

Functional programming is another programming paradigm, just as OOP is a paradigm. It is the concept of accepting functions as arguments and being able to return functions as a result (known as *higher-order functions*). This approach is very powerful, and many JavaScript libraries take advantage of JavaScript's capability to do this.

Callbacks

A *callback* is the process of passing in a function (or the name of a function) into another function so that when the code finishes executing, it can "call that function back." Callbacks are quite common, especially in event-driven scenarios. In fact, most custom event systems use callbacks as a way of calling a function when an event occurs.

Callbacks are normally handled by passing a function into another object as one of the parameters:

```
function Animation(startFunction, endFunction)
{
    startFunction();
    /* perform our animation magic here */
    endFunction();
}

Animation( function(){ alert('Start!') }, function(){ alert('End!') } );
```

Two anonymous functions were passed in: the first will get called before the animation starts; the second will get called after it ends.

Passing in a function that is a method of an object can be problematic unless
what to expect. In this case, the method will be disconnected from the object. Whe
tion is executed from within the other function, you'll likely get an error message:

```
function Pizza(includePepperoni)
```

```
...ludePepperoni;
                              ... this.pepperoni; }
```

...e key thing to note is that the ingredient
...as become detached from the newPizza
...t of the eatPizza() function, which happens
...peroni property.
...o run the function in the context of another
...asIngredient, which is the function
...ns it in the context of the pizza, which is the
...aves just like newPizza.hasPepperoni(). The
... now properly tells you whether there is pep-

```
...t.call(pizza) );
```

```
za );
```

...ures to pass the information in by using your origi-

```
    alert('Has Ingredi...          dient() );
}
```

```
eatPizza( function(){ return newPizza.hasPepperoni() } );
```

An anonymous function was passed in that simply returns whether the value is true or
false. As you've no doubt discovered, there's almost always more than one way to accomplish
the same thing.

The Functions call and apply

As you just saw, you can use `call` to run a function as if it were attached to a particular object. You can also specify any number of additional parameters that should be passed on to the function:

```
hasIngredient.call(pizza, 'hot');
```

This behaves the same as if you did the following:

```
newPizza.hasPepperoni('hot');
```

The `apply` function works almost the same way, but instead of specifying each parameter separately, you can pass in an array as the second parameter, and each of those parameters is passed through to the function in the same order as specified in the array:

```
hasIngredient.apply(pizza, ['hot','medium','mild']);
```

This behaves the same as if you did the following:

```
newPizza.hasPepperoni('hot','medium','mild');
```

The Prototype JavaScript library has probably one of the most applicable applications of the `apply` function. It extends the `Function` prototype so every function can automatically be bound to an object with a very succinct syntax:

```
Function.prototype.bind = function() {
  var __method = this, args = $A(arguments), object = args.shift();
  return function() {
    return __method.apply(object, args.concat($A(arguments)));
  }
}
```

The `$A` function is a Prototype JavaScript library function that takes a collection and turns it into an array by iterating over the collection and adding each element into the array. It then uses the array method `shift` to knock off the first element in the array and save it. This is the first parameter you pass into the function and is the object with which you want to bind. Next, it returns an anonymous function that does the fun stuff. Through the closure, it takes the current function, which was assigned to __method, and applies it to `object`. It then takes the arguments from before and adds them to the current list of arguments.

Here's an example that demonstrates the relationship between everything:

```
function ObjectA(){ /* stuff */ }
ObjectA.methodB = function ()
{
  // arguments now has 6 elements:
  alert($A(arguments)); // 1,2,3,4,5,6
}

var bound = ObjectA.methodB.bind(ObjectA, '1','2','3','4');
bound('5','6');
```

Using `call` or `apply`, especially as shown here, can make your code look cleaner and more readable.

Applying a Function to a Collection

A handy way to use callbacks is to apply a function to a series of elements within an array or object (which are very similar in functionality). The ability to receive functions as parameters enables you to apply a function to any and all items within a collection.

Here's a great example taken from jQuery (http://jquery.com):

```
$("p").each(function(){
    this.innerHTML = this + " is the Element";
  });
```

Despite the brevity of this code example, there's actually a lot happening here. First, a function called $() takes in a string parameter. In this case, it finds all <p> elements on the page. In other words, $("p") returns a collection of paragraphs in the document. Then, the each() method will apply a function to each item in the collection (in this case, the innerHTML of each paragraph tag will be replaced with the string).

You can create your own example now that will parse through your own special array:

```
function SpecialArray(arr)
{
  this.arr = arr;
}
SpecialArray.prototype.map = function(func)
{
   for(var i = 0; i < this.arr.length; i++)
   {
    this.arr[i] = func(this.arr[i]);
   }
   return this;
}

var obj = new SpecialArray( ['A','B','C'] );
obj.map( function(el){ return el.toLowerCase() } ); // returns ['a','b','c']
```

First, there is a special new object called SpecialArray that has an internal array and one method called map(). The map() method takes a function and runs that function on each of the elements within the array. In this case, it changes all the elements from uppercase to lowercase. By keeping it agnostic like this, you can manipulate the elements in the array any way you please by simply passing in a different function:

```
obj.map( function(el){ return el + '!' } ); // returns ['A!','B!','C!']
```

You can even work with arrays of different object types:

```
var obj = new SpecialArray( [1,2,3] );
obj.map( function(el){ return el * el } ); // returns [1,4,9]
```

Chainable Methods

You've seen plenty of examples that follow the `object.method()` approach to things. However, it can become cumbersome to assign something to a variable only to have to manipulate the object further. Instead, you can often keep your code looking cleaner and simpler by chaining methods together. This is quite common when working with string methods like this example:

```
"I went to my store".toUpperCase().replace("MY", "YOUR");
// returns "I WENT TO YOUR STORE"
```

With each method returning a string, you can continue to manipulate that string by adding on new methods. If you begin chaining a lot of methods, you can make the code cleaner by putting each subsequent call onto its own line:

```
"I went to my store"
   .toUpperCase()
   .replace("MY", "YOUR");
// returns "I WENT TO YOUR STORE"
```

To create your own chainable methods, you simply have to ensure that you are always returning something at the end of a method call. With that returned data, you can continue to manipulate it.

Using the `SpecialArray`, you can continue to manipulate the array with subsequent map calls because you return the `SpecialArray` on which you're performing the map:

```
var obj = new SpecialArray( ['A','B','C'] );
var arr = obj
  .map( function(el){ return el.toLowerCase() } ) // returns ['a','b','c']
  .map( function(el){ return el += '!' } ); // returns ['a!','b!','c!']
```

Internal Iterators

Collections are quite common in DOM scripting—from a simple array to a node list returned from a `getElementsByTagName()` call. Creating a class—or extending the ones built into JavaScript—can give you added flexibility to be able to manipulate those collections. An *internal iterator* is a mechanism that enables you to navigate through a collection using exposed elements.

Here's an example collection object that enables you to navigate:

```
function Collection (arr)
{
  this.current = 0;
  this.items = arr;
}

Collection.prototype.getCurrent = function()
{
  return this.items[this.current];
}
```

```
Collection.prototype.getNext = function()
{
  return this.items[++this.current];
}
Collection.prototype.getPrevious = function()
{
  return this.items[--this.current];
}

var coll = new Collection( [1,2,3,4] );
alert( coll.getCurrent() ); // 1
alert( coll.getNext() ); // on to 2
alert( coll.getPrevious() ); // back to 1
```

You have your main `Collection` class, which stores a pointer to the current item and the array in a property called `items`. The `getCurrent()`, `getNext()`, and `getPrevious()` methods enable you to move back and forth within the array, constantly updating the `current` pointer. It could be extended with the `map()` function you saw earlier, along with error detection to check whether you have reached the end or beginning of the collection.

Many of the JavaScript libraries have implemented iterators and offer plenty of methods that can be extremely handy in working with collections of data like this.

Summary

In this chapter, you got a good sense of some object-oriented programming using JavaScript. Some of the things you should know before you move on include the following:

- The different ways to create objects and when it is beneficial to use one instead of another

- How to extend objects with methods and properties and when to use the prototype property

- How to take advantage of closures

- How to use callbacks

Chapter 4 dives into the wonderful world of JavaScript libraries to learn what they have to offer, and why and how you should use them.

CHAPTER 4

■ ■ ■

Libraries

JavaScript libraries have been around in one form or another for almost as long as JavaScript itself. As you go from project to project, it's inevitable that you'll find yourself reusing various functions. They become part of your core that you end up copying each time you start up something new. With any good library, code reuse leads to reliability; using the same code on multiple projects means that the code has been exposed to more and more people, enabling bugs or cross-browser issues to be resolved.

You can, of course, use someone else's library. Using an existing library such as Prototype or jQuery gives you a higher level of reliability that might be difficult to attain through maintaining your own code base.

The trade-off of using a library is file size. Some of these libraries, if taken as a whole, weigh in at more than 300 kilobytes. However, library developers are tuned in to these kinds of issues and are building their code in a very modular way, enabling you to pick and choose only the features you need. This keeps the amount of code bloat to a minimum. Sites such as Mootools.net even include a module picker that enables you to select whether to compress the files or not.

Libraries serve a number of purposes, which I've summarized into three categories:

- Document object model (DOM) access, traversing, and manipulation

- Application conveniences including language extensions

- Widgets

Working with the DOM

Because you're working with HTML and Cascading Style Sheets (CSS), the DOM is likely the most important interface when it comes to a solid library. It not only improves your efficiency at retrieving elements from the DOM but it also smoothes the bumps of manipulation and traversal that tend to be inconsistent across browsers.

Many of today's popular libraries include some methods for working with the DOM, including the capability to select nodes via CSS selectors and to move through a collection of nodes using functions such as `nextSibling()` and `previousSibling()`. They often have conveniences for inserting new elements into the DOM, which is a tiresome process at best.

Animation

Part of working with the DOM is handling animation. Being able to handle animation means being able to read and modify several DOM properties, such as the `style` object and element offsets. Animation is simply the manipulation of element properties over time. It's also a great way to add interest to a page and can improve the usability of your site or application if used appropriately. (You'll learn more about animation in Chapter 6.)

Application Conveniences

The desktop is slowly moving to the Web with applications such as Google Docs and Spreadsheets, and Google Mail. With these types of applications you are working not only with the DOM but also with large data sets. JavaScript has some basic mechanisms, including arrays and simple iteration, for handling data sets. However, larger data sets often require filtering and ways to quickly load that data into the DOM.

Libraries solve these problems by automating much of the tedium as well as providing a unified application programming interface (API) to various JavaScript and DOM features. Libraries address the following issues:

- Language extensions and bridges

- Event handling

- Ajax

- Strings and templating

- Working with collections

- Handling JSON and XML

Language Extensions and Bridges

JavaScript and the DOM are great, but (as you saw in the last chapter) they weren't necessarily designed to do certain things (for example, deep inheritance, in which one object inherits from another, which inherits from another, and so on). Similarly, new language features get implemented in some browsers, but take a while before being introduced into other browsers. These features can be covered with a *language bridge*, which is a chunk of code that makes the feature of one browser available in another browser. A great example is the `Array.push()` method. Older browser versions such as Internet Explorer (IE) version 5 didn't support it. A simple function such as the following would be used to bridge the gap between the support in IE 5 and other more modern browsers:

```
// if the method doesn't exist then add it in
if (!Array.prototype.push) {
   Array.prototype.push = function(obj) {
      this[this.length] = obj;
   }
}
```

Event Handling

Event handling falls under the category of "Language Extensions and Bridges," but I separated it into its own section because it's so important. Far above any other issue, event handling is the biggest problem that web developers using JavaScript have to deal with. Libraries solve this problem by creating a unified interface for attaching events, maintaining object scope, and stopping events. Let's take a look at an example from Prototype:

```
Event.observe(element, 'click',
    (function(){ alert(this.href) }).bindAsEventListener(element)
    );
```

In Prototype an `Event` object has an `observe()` method that enables you to observe events on a particular object. You want to track a click event on an element (a link, in this case). The third parameter enables you to pass in a function to be called when the event is fired. Because this is a simple example, I created an anonymous function, but notice the method `bindAsEventListener()`. This method takes a single parameter: the element that should have scope from within the function. When the function gets called, `this` will refer to `element`. The `bindAsEventListener()` method makes use of the `apply()` method (refer to Chapter 3), which ensures that scope is maintained.

Ajax

Ajax originally stood for Asynchronous JavaScript and XML, but it has morphed into an umbrella term that encapsulates a number of technologies. At the core of Ajax, though, is still the idea of using JavaScript to communicate with the server to send and receive data without having to refresh the page. This is done using the `XMLHttpRequest` object, often referred to as the XHR object.

The XHR object was originally created by Microsoft as an ActiveX object back in 2000. Mozilla went on to create a native implementation of XHR in 2002; since then, Safari and Opera have added support for it.

Ajax in itself is fairly straightforward, but handling all the contingencies might not be obvious. JavaScript libraries provide a framework for handling successful calls and problem calls (timeouts, for example). Chapter 5 will discuss Ajax in more detail.

Strings and Templating

When you work with Ajax-based web applications, you frequently take data that has been received from the server and place it on the page somehow. The quickest way to do it is to receive a full HTML snippet from the server and just plunk it on the page. However, that process isn't very practical. You end up using a lot of bandwidth just to send a little bit of data. *Templating* solves this problem by enabling data received from the server to be quickly merged with a template and then embedded in the page.

Additionally, web programming constantly uses strings, and having ways to filter, capitalize, or camel case strings can be extremely handy.

Here's an example using Prototype to combine a data set with a template to create a list of links:

```
<ul id="myul"></ul>

<script type="text/javascript">
var ul = $('myul');
//the dataset
var linkdata = [{name: 'About', url: '/about/'},
    {name: 'Contact', url: '/contact/'},
    {name: 'Help', url: '/help/'}];

//the template
var templ = new Template('<a href="#{url}">#{name}</a>');

//let's add each of these to the document.
linkdata.each( function(conv){
    li = document.createElement('li');
    li.innerHTML = templ.evaluate(conv);
    ul.appendChild(li);
});
</script>
```

The example starts with an empty unordered list retrieved using the Prototype dollar function $(). After that, some link information, which is a normal array of object literals, is declared. Next, a new string template, which is another feature of Prototype, is declared. The link data goes through each one using the Prototype each() method. Prototype automatically makes the each() method available on all arrays. Each item in the array is evaluated into the template and spit into a new list item, which gets appended to the list. In this case, the link data is embedded in the script. A more common scenario is to pull in the link data via an Ajax call.

Working with Collections

A *collection* is an array of objects, and the array functionality within JavaScript can be limiting. Prototype, for example, includes a very robust Enumerable class for working with collections. You can use methods that will automatically scan the array and remove elements, add elements, or return only a subset of elements.

As you saw in the last example, the each() method on the array was used to loop through the array. Iteration is much simpler than having to create for loops every time.

Handling JSON and XML

The need to handle data sets is tied mostly to Ajax. These data sets need to be transferred in a format that enables you to quickly understand how the data is structured. The two most popular ways to do this are by using JSON and XML.

JSON (http://json.org), which stands for JavaScript Object Notation, uses a subset of JavaScript to safely define and transport data. JSON parsers are available for dozens of server-side languages, making it extremely easy to integrate into a project. JSON has slowly been taking over XML in popularity for transporting data from the server side to the client side for a couple of reasons:

- JSON is almost always smaller in size because less markup is needed to define the data.

- JSON is quicker to parse and use on the client side because it is native JavaScript.

XML support was built into the `responseXML` property of the original XHR object being returned. With an XML object, you can use familiar DOM methods to traverse the XML.

JavaScript libraries make handling JSON and XML easier by being able to automatically detect which type of data is being returned by an XHR call and parse it appropriately. With JSON, the data can be parsed to prevent against invalid or dangerous information being served up from the server.

Widgets

Widgets are prebuilt components (such as file browsers, tabbed interfaces, or custom dialogs) that can be plugged into an application and solve a discrete task, as can be seen in Figure 4-1. Widgets essentially combine the first two categories—DOM manipulation and application conveniences—into a well-oiled machine. Prebuilt widgets are best used for solving common design issues and can take the pain out of having to deal with complicated edge cases that inevitably occur when building complicated interfaces.

Figure 4-1. *An example page from the ExtJS library featuring a tree widget, layout elements, and drag and drop*

Popular Libraries

A few libraries were previously mentioned, but brace yourself. Hundreds of libraries are out there doing seemingly identical things, with more coming out almost daily. Each library might take a slightly different approach to a certain feature—depending on what that developer felt was important to include.

Thankfully, there's plenty of support—including from large corporations—for just a handful of libraries, each with its own strengths and weaknesses. Weaknesses tend to be addressed quickly by using techniques used by competing libraries or through plug-ins.

One of the largest downfalls of many open-source movements is documentation. You'll certainly find that documentation can be sparse and unclear. Some libraries do a better job than others at addressing this.

The current leaders of the pack are the following:

- Dojo

- Prototype

- jQuery

- Yahoo! UI Library (YUI)

- Mootools

Library plug-ins focused specifically on animation or widgets include the following:

- Script.aculo.us

- Interface

- ExtJS

Recent additions likely to become popular include the following:

- base2.DOM

- DED|Chain

Let's discuss each library in more detail to see how it can be used in your next project.

Dojo

Dojo (http://dojotoolkit.com) is a large library focused on easing the web application development process by having widgets and other interface elements easily dropped into any project. Here's a description from the Dojo web site:

> *Dojo enables you to easily build dynamic capabilities into web pages and any other environment that supports JavaScript sanely. You can use the components that Dojo provides to make your web sites more usable, responsive, and functional. With Dojo you can build degradable user interfaces more easily, prototype interactive widgets quickly, and animate transitions.*

The Dojo library focuses on creating a platform on which to build desktop-like web applications like the e-mail example shown in Figure 4-2. It can be daunting and would certainly be overkill if all you ever need to do is add some animation to your blog.

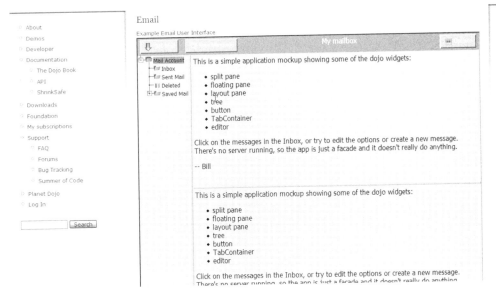

Figure 4-2. *A Dojo example that uses many of the widgets available within the toolkit*

Dojo covers all three of the key areas that libraries attempt to address: it smoothes the rough terrain of working with the DOM, it includes many application conveniences, and it includes many prebuilt widgets.

Prototype

Prototype (http://prototypejs.org) was one of the first libraries to gain widespread popularity and helped popularize many of the JavaScript techniques used today. Prototype was originally designed by Sam Stephenson (http://conio.net) and integrated into Ruby on Rails (http://www.rubyonrails.org). Many of the ways that Prototype approaches problems are similar in style to Ruby.

One of the reasons for Prototype's popularity is the way it makes many things much easier, including the infamous dollar sign function (\$). By using the dollar sign function, methods are automatically attached to the returned DOM element, adding a lot more power to what you can do with an element. Recent iterations of the library have improved on method chaining, making it a formidable tool:

```
$('elementId').show(); // shows an element that was hidden using display:none
```

Prototype, unlike other libraries, really focuses heavily on addressing two key areas: working with the DOM and application conveniences including lots of string functions, and a custom enumeration object that is used to extend a custom hash object and the built-in `Array` object. When it comes to building web applications—especially Ajax-driven ones—Prototype is a solid solution.

The latest version of Prototype also features a double dollar function ($$) for using CSS selectors to retrieve an array of elements. Here's a great example of how easy it can be used to create an expand and collapse feature for an FAQ page:

```
<div class="question">What is an apple?</div>
<div class="answer">It's a fruit!</div>

$$('.question').each(function(el){
    Event.observe(el , 'click', (function(){
      this.next().toggle()
    }).bindAsEventListener(el));
});
```

There's a bunch of things happening in this example. First is the $$() function, which retrieves any element on the page with a class name of question. This function returns an array of elements. Because it is an array, you can now use the Array.each() method that the Prototype library makes available to you. It takes a function as its sole parameter, executing it for each element in the array, with the element getting passed into that function.

Within that anonymous function, a click event handler is attached to each element. The element is bound as the event listener to access it from within the event handler by using the this keyword. When a user clicks a question, the function will grab the next element and toggle its visibility.

With this level of succinctness, you can lose readability. There are ways to write the code to make it easier to read, but it's often at the cost of brevity. Here's a quick example that uses named functions instead of anonymous functions to improve readability:

```
function onEach(el)
{
    function toggle()
    {
        this.next().toggle();
    }
    Event.observe(el, 'click', toggle.bindAsEventListener(el));
}
$$('.question').each( onEach );
```

Prototype's approach to object-oriented design is firmly in the object literal camp. A constructor can be created by specifying an initializing function:

```
<input type="text" id="searchfield" value="Search">

<script type="text/javascript">
var FormField = Class.create();
FormField.prototype = {
  initialize: function(id) {
    var el = $(id);
    Event.observe(el,'focus',(function()
```

```
   {
       if(this.value == this.defaultValue) this.value = '';
   }).bindAsEventListener(el));

   Event.observe(el,'blur',(function()
   {
       if(this.value == '') this.value = this.defaultValue;
   }).bindAsEventListener(el));
  }
};

new FormField('searchfield');
</script>
```

This example used the Prototype method of creating a class and then attaching the `initialize()` function to the prototype by specifying it as a method in the object literal. When a new object is instantiated from it, the `initialize()` function is automatically run. The focus and blur events are observed. For the focus event, if the value contained within is the default value, it will clear the input, enabling the user to type from scratch. Then, on blur, the field is reset to the default value if the field is blank.

jQuery

jQuery (http://jquery.com) is quick and nimble, and it was the first library that really high-lighted the power of method chaining. The library is well encapsulated and is guaranteed to play well with other libraries using its own `jQuery` namespace. It offers a dollar sign function that maps to an internal method. If you are using jQuery alongside Prototype or another library that makes use of the dollar function, you can turn it off in jQuery.

jQuery is compact, yet extremely powerful. However, it is light in features when it comes to many of the tasks required to handle desktop-like functionality in a web application. There's no templating or the capability to work with data sets from within the library. If you need to add some interactivity to your site, jQuery is a great solution.

Here's a quick example that helps demonstrate where jQuery really shines:

```
$("p.surprise").addClass("ohmy").show("slow");
```

You can probably see many similarities between this example and that for Prototype. First and foremost, the important thing is how the dollar sign function accepts CSS selectors; with Prototype you have to use the double dollar sign function. If you end up using each of these libraries on different projects, this mistake might trip you up from time to time.

After the elements are retrieved, the example adds a class name of `ohmy` to each of the elements. After that, the `show()` method animates the elements. In this case, the script will create a slow slide out on each paragraph with a class name of `surprise`.

Event handling is similarly done with method chaining. In the following example, all paragraph elements on the page are retrieved. Each one gets a click event attached to it. When the event fires, it will retrieve the text from that element. The `text()` method is a method of the jQuery object.

```
$("p").bind("click", function(){
  alert( $(this).text() );
});
```

Chaining works so well because jQuery returns a jQuery object each time. In fact, $() is really just a shortcut to the jQuery function. The function uses itself as a class to instantiate new objects from itself each time it is run. In doing so, the jQuery object can be accessed much like a singleton (as in the following example) or as an object generator (as in the preceding examples). This example instantiates an Ajax request and grabs the responseText property from that, assigning it to a variable (check out Chapter 5 for more information on how Ajax works):

```
var html = $.ajax({
  url: "/servercall/",
  async: false
}).responseText;
```

For documentation on jQuery, visit http://docs.jquery.com.

Yahoo! UI Library (YUI)

YUI (http://developer.yahoo.com/yui) is developed and backed by the folks at Yahoo! It's used on many of the Yahoo! properties, so it's well designed and extremely robust. YUI takes a more traditional approach to its library design—each method is simply a function call that takes a number of parameters. You don't get method chaining as with jQuery or the conveniences of many of the functions within Prototype (but take a look at DED|chain, mentioned later in this chapter, which extends YUI to include method chaining). What you do get is a well-thought-out library and prebuilt functionality that goes beyond many of the libraries mentioned in this chapter.

YUI is also heavily namespaced. There's the main YAHOO object; then everything branches off from there. For example, to retrieve an element via the identifier, use the following:

```
YAHOO.util.Dom.get('elementID');
```

Of the three categories of problems that libraries try to solve, YUI mostly tackles DOM tools such as those offered up in the Dom namespace and the Anim namespace (for animation). It also includes a number of widgets, such as those shown in Figure 4-3.

Figure 4-3. *The TreeView, TabView, and Calendar controls available within the YUI library*

Using the widgets can be a handy way to add complex functionality into an application. The calendar widget is a very common one that can be used easily as a date picker:

```
function selEvent(type, args)
{
  // type = event type ='select'

  // the date selected is the first element in the array
  var dates = args[0];
  // the date clicked on is the first element of that array
  var date = dates[0];
  // the date is stored in an array as [YYYYY, MM, DD]
  var year = date[0], month = date[1], day = date[2];
}
widget = new YAHOO.widget.Calendar("cal1","calwidget",{close:true,iframe:true});
widget.selectEvent.subscribe(selEvent, this, true);
widget.render();
```

The calendar widget takes three parameters: the first parameter is a unique identifier for the calendar itself, the second is the ID of the HTML element being used as the placeholder for the widget, and the third is an object literal to store options. In this case, you want to show a CLOSE button and use an `<iframe>`, which sits behind the calendar and is used to lie on top of `<select>` boxes that don't allow other HTML elements to be shown over them. This issue mostly applies to IE 6 or less; it has been fixed in IE 7.

Although the excessive namespacing might seem like a hassle, there's always a really quick way to create a shortcut. The following mimics Prototype a little bit by declaring a dollar sign function on the page and points it to the `get()` method of the `Dom` object:

```
var $ = YAHOO.util.Dom.get;
var el = $('elementID');
```

Using the encapsulation techniques described in Chapter 3, you can create the shortcuts within function calls or classes to keep the global namespace as clean as possible.

Mootools

Mootools (http://mootools.net) is a relative newcomer to the library scene. It originally started as Moo.fx, which was an effects library built on top of the Prototype library. The developers behind it felt they had an opportunity to build a compact and modular library. One of the major benefits of Mootools is the download configurator (see Figure 4-4), which enables you to select which modules of the library you need. You can also choose the level of compression that should be performed. All the dependencies between the modules are determined automatically. You can also decide whether to use a compressed version of the library or one that is fully documented. By using a minimized version of the code, you can reduce the file size and thereby reduce the amount of bandwidth the file needs to use. Many of the other libraries, such as jQuery and YUI, also offer up minimized versions.

Figure 4-4. *Mootools download configurator*

Note During the development phase of a project, it's best to use the uncompressed versions of the libraries. Debugging is much easier because code becomes easier to trace when in an unminimized form. In its current 1.05 version, Firebug might report incorrect function names when using a minimized form. Just remember to switch to the compressed versions when you're ready to launch.

One of my favorite features of Mootools is its capability to not only set animation on an element but to set it on multiple elements at one time:

```
var myElementsEffects = new Fx.Elements($$('a'));
myElementsEffects.start({
  '0': { //let's change the first element's opacity and width
    'opacity': [0,1],
    'width': [100,200]
  },
  '4': { //and the fifth one's opacity
    'opacity': [0.2, 0.5]
  }
});
```

Using the Fx.Elements class, it uses the $$() function just like Prototype; in this case, it passes in a list of links. The start() method starts the animation and takes an options object as its only parameter. The object literal uses keys to define which elements should be animated. The first and fifth elements (you're starting from 0) will be animated with the first element having its opacity changed from 0 percent to 100 percent (going from invisible to completely visible) and its width going from 100px to 200px. The fifth element has its opacity changed from 20 percent to 50 percent.

This functionality is handy if you have a number of dependent animations, such as having one area expand while a number of other areas collapse at the same time.

Script.aculo.us

Script.aculo.us (http://script.aculo.us) is an animation and widget library built on top of Prototype. The Prototype/Script.aculo.us combo is quite popular and is the default in a number of server-side frameworks.

Effects can be quickly and easily applied by using a couple lines of code:

```
new Effect.Opacity('myElement',
    { duration: 2.0,
      transition: Effect.Transitions.linear,
      from: 1.0, to: 0.5 });
```

The class takes the element ID (or the element itself) as the first parameter and an options object literal as the second parameter. This example changes the opacity of an element from 100 percent to 50 percent over 2 seconds. The transition property enables mathematical transitions to be applied to create a more natural feel to the animations. They can start off slow and then speed up. They can start off fast and then slow down. They can even bounce back and forth before settling into place.

Script.aculo.us really shines when you use its controls, making it super simple to add them in any project. Here's a sortable list example:

```
Sortable.create("firstlist",
    {dropOnEmpty:true,
     containment:["firstlist","secondlist"],
     constraint:false});
```

The Sortable control expects to use a list by default and makes each element draggable, which enables each element to be dragged elsewhere in the tree (enabling the user to re-sort the items). You can even enable dragging and dropping between lists. In this example, the control enables elements to be dragged between firstlist and secondlist.

ExtJS

ExtJS (http://extjs.com) is a widget library, but it surpasses all others mentioned here in its elegance and flexibility. It used to go under the name YUI.Ext because it was specifically an add-on to the YUI library (just as Script.aculo.us is for Prototype). However, as the extension neared its 1.0 release, the add-on got reworked to enable ExtJS to work with YUI, jQuery, or Prototype. Now in its 1.1 release, ExtJS includes a stand-alone version, removing the need for other libraries.

The documentation for the library even uses its own components, including the Tree and Layout widgets, as seen in Figure 4-5.

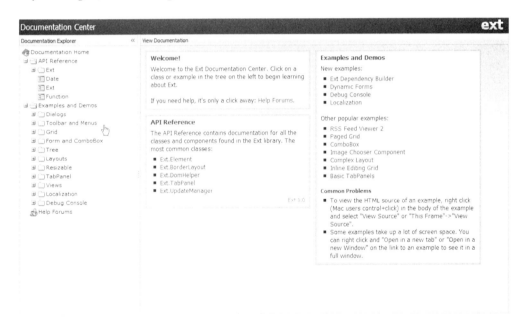

Figure 4-5. *ExtJS documentation using ExtJS widgets*

ExtJS is fantastic for application prototyping because of the ease in which many of the features can be implemented. The file browser–style navigation on the left side seen in Figure 4-5 is easily created using a few lines of code:

```
Ext.onReady(function(){
    // shorthand
    var Tree = Ext.tree;
```

```
    var tree = new Tree.TreePanel('tree-div', {
        animate:true,
        loader: new Tree.TreeLoader({
            dataUrl:'get-nodes.php'
        }),
        enableDD:true,
        containerScroll: true
    });

    // set the root node
    var root = new Tree.AsyncTreeNode({
        text: 'Ext JS',
        draggable:false,
        id:'source'
    });
    tree.setRootNode(root);

    // render the tree
    tree.render();
    root.expand();
});
```

Ext.js has an onReady() function that runs a piece of code as soon as the DOM is ready, which normally occurs well before the window.onload event fires. jQuery has a similar function, as does Prototype via Dan Webb's LowPro plug-in available at http://www.danwebb.net/lowpro.

The tree structure is handled via a number of objects in the Ext.tree namespace: TreePanel, TreeLoader, and AsyncTreeNode. The TreePanel takes two parameters: the first is the ID in which the panel should be embedded, and the second is an object literal for options. One of those options is loader, which uses the TreeLoader object to load in objects from the server. In this example, the data is to be loaded as a JSON object from a PHP script.

A new node is created and set as the root node of the tree panel. The node is rendered and then set to expand. By expanding the node, it will load in the child nodes using the TreeLoader object. Once the data is loaded, it is cached on the client side so that further collapse/expands don't continually make calls to the server.

The tree nodes are very extensible and enable additional attributes to be attached to them. The look of the nodes can also be completely customized, as demonstrated in Figure 4-6.

The ExtJS library includes widgets for custom dialogs (instead of using alerts or pop-up windows), tabbed interfaces, data grids, layouts, and a whole lot more.

ExtJS is also more than just a widget library because many of the underlying components to these widgets can be used on their own as application conveniences such as the built-in DOM tools, the event handling, the state management classes, or the data format classes for XML or JSON handling.

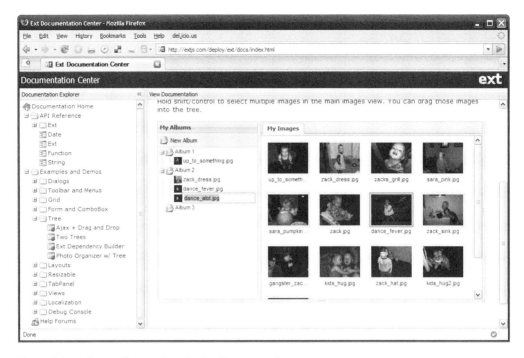

Figure 4-6. *A photo album using the ExtJS* TreePanel

New Libraries

Of course, nobody is ever content to leave well enough alone—and probably for good reason. Libraries are continually tweaked and added upon to meet the needs of the ever-growing number of people using these libraries. Inevitably, some will attempt to make their own library to address the needs that libraries before them haven't met.

Base2.DOM

Dean Edwards, a man who has contributed heavily to the popularity of JavaScript (including his IE7Scripts that aim to fix CSS issues in IE 6 and IE 7), has come up with his own DOM tools (http://dean.edwards.name/weblog/2007/03/yet-another).

Dean takes a different approach to developing a library: build an API that matches that of the World Wide Web Consortium (W3C) and JavaScript 1.5 (http://developer.mozilla.org/en/docs/Core_JavaScript_1.5_Reference), the idea being to support features such as addEventListener() or Array.forEach() that some browsers don't yet support (but hopefully will). As new browsers come online that support these features, that portion of the library becomes no longer necessary, yet no code that depended on the library has to change.

DED|Chain

As mentioned, YUI doesn't support method chaining. Many of those who have come to appreciate jQuery's simplicity have found YUI to be cumbersome to work with. Dustin Diaz developed DED|Chain (`http://dedchain.dustindiaz.com`) to fill that gap by taking the YUI library and extending it to offer chainable methods such as the following:

```
_$('#elementID').on('click', function(){ /* code goes here */ });
```

This uses `_$` much as jQuery uses the `$` to enable the retrieval of DOM elements using CSS selectors. In this case, it returns all objects with an ID of `elementID` (you should have only one) and then attaches an onclick event handler to them.

DED|Chain is still early in development, but I want to point it out because it emphasizes one of the key features of JavaScript: it's extremely flexible. Code can easily be extended to offer the features that the core library might not take into account.

How to Choose a Library

With so many libraries out there and so many more to come, how can you ever narrow down the field? Of course, your choice depends entirely on what you need to accomplish. As discussed at the beginning of this chapter, libraries tend to fall into one of the three major categories: DOM tool, application helper, or widget. You need to consider what you might be building and narrow down the field from there.

If you just need to add some interactivity to your blog, such as simple slide effects, you'll want a library that focuses on the core DOM features along with some basic effects. Mootools or jQuery, for example, might be a good fit.

If you want to build a web application and need to manipulate data sets along with prototyping a complex user interface, using Prototype along with ExtJS might be a better solution.

When looking at any library, be sure to get your hands dirty and take a look at the source. You'll need to have a good understanding of how the library is put together to be able to take advantage of its power. Plus, it'll make it easier to do apples-to-apples comparisons.

The Community

Do a search in your favorite search engine to see who's using the library and the types of things they run into. Having a popular community behind it is a good indication of how solid a library it is. You'll also find places you can visit, such as blogs and forums, if you ever run into a problem.

The Documentation

With many libraries being built and maintained by only a small team of developers on their own time, you can imagine that documentation falls to the bottom of the to-do list. For example, this was an issue with the Prototype library until only recently. The library had no documentation except for a few third-party resources. A team of individuals banded together to ensure that the library development itself continued on and that a proper site be built in its honor, along with documentation.

Tip When picking a library, be sure to look through the documentation. Is it up to date? Does it have proper examples?

Luckily, as more and more people develop on top of these libraries, more examples will make their way onto the Internet, and the documentation will be added to. JavaScript libraries are almost always open-source projects that invite you to contribute to the active development of the library.

Summary

You discovered that the field is ripe for the picking, with any number of JavaScript libraries that might be well suited for your next project. It's not necessary to reinvent the wheel each time. The libraries mentioned in this chapter are popular, which means they are getting used by thousands (even millions) of people, and that kind of quality assurance is hard to beat if you're continually starting from scratch. This will save plenty of time, not only in the development of consistent cross-browser code but also with the bug testing and maintenance of such. Each library has its strengths and weaknesses, and picking the right tool for the job can sometimes be half the battle.

Next up, you'll look at Ajax and after that Visual Effects. In both chapters and the case studies to follow, you'll see the topic of JavaScript libraries come up again and see some great examples of how they can be applied to a project.

CHAPTER 5

■ ■ ■

Ajax and Data Exchange

If you've heard the term used only casually, you might have pondered whether *Ajax* has simply become the new word for *JavaScript*. The term, coined by Jesse James Garrett of Adaptive Path, actually came about fairly recently (in 2005). Garrett (and probably others within Adaptive Path) came up with the term as a convenient way of describing a specific interaction: Asynchronous JavaScript and XML.

With Ajax, JavaScript can communicate with the server, returning results in a chunk of XML. You can then use that new data to update what the user sees on the screen, and it all is done without a page refresh. The great thing about this process is the asynchronous part: you can perform these tasks behind the scenes while the user continues to interact with the page at hand.

This chapter covers the following:

- Deconstructing the Ajax process

- Understanding data formats

- Building a reusable Ajax object

- Using libraries to handle Ajax calls

First, however, let's look at a good example of Ajax and how it achieves the effects it does.

Examining an Ajax Application

Google Docs & Spreadsheets—along with most of the Google online applications, for that matter—demonstrates the power of Ajax very well (see Figure 5-1). Changes to your document get constantly sent back to the server to be saved. This type of interaction is just like using a desktop application such as Microsoft Word. And although many of the applications that make use of the technique attempt to be like desktop applications, it can be used for even small tasks that can make a site seem extremely responsive and fun to use.

As another example, take a look at Figure 5-2. Notice the star where you can highlight a particularly interesting item. Traditionally, clicking it would require the entire page to be reloaded (all 16KB of it, not including JavaScript, Cascading Style Sheets [CSS], and images). With Ajax, the user never leaves the spot, and the interaction sends only a few bytes back and forth.

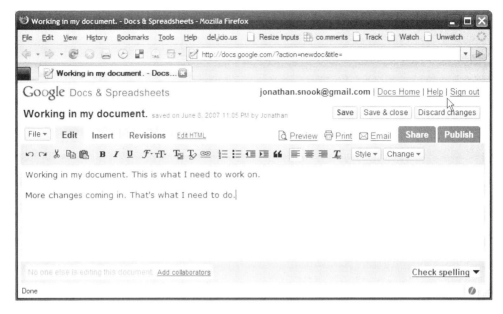

Figure 5-1. *Google Docs automatically saves changes every minute to prevent losing any precious changes.*

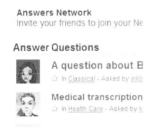

Figure 5-2. *The star enables you to target this item as interesting without having to refresh the page.*

Deconstructing the Ajax Process

At the core of Ajax is the XMLHttpRequest object (which is often referred to as XHR). Microsoft originally developed an ActiveX object to be used for Outlook Web Access way back in 2000. However, without cross-browser support, the functionality remained mostly in obscurity. When Mozilla implemented a native version of the object in its browser, things really began to take hold. Finally, with Safari and Opera implementing it, it took off. Now there are entire conferences and consortia based on this lovely word.

While Ajax described a very specific set of interactions, its meaning has expanded somewhat to include a broader concept: any communication to the server via JavaScript using the XMLHttpRequest object. The data returned might be XML, but it could also be HTML, JSON, CSV, or whatever text format your heart desires.

The process of making an Ajax request is fairly straightforward. Here's a quick example put together for you:

```
// Use the native version for everybody but IE6<
if(window.XMLHttpRequest) {
    transport = new XMLHttpRequest();
}else{
    try{ transport = new ActiveXObject("MSXML2.XMLHTTP.6.0");  }catch(e){}
    try{ transport = new ActiveXObject("MSXML2.XMLHTTP");  }catch(e){}
}

if(transport)
{
    transport.open("GET", "http://example.com/test/", true);
    transport.onreadystatechange = function(){ alert('I am back!'); };
    transport.send();
}
```

This is the basic structure of an Ajax request. The first part instantiates the XHR object, beginning with trying to instantiate a native version of the object. If a native implementation is not found, it attempts to instantiate the ActiveX objects for Internet Explorer (IE). (You'll learn more about why we check for both implementations later on.)

The second part takes the object and opens a connection with three parameters: the first specifies the method (GET or POST), the second is the URL you want to open, and the third determines whether the call should be synchronous or asynchronous.

If the third parameter is set to synchronous (false), the browser will wait for the call to return before users can do anything. This isn't ideal because users might think their browser has frozen and needs to be shut down. Setting it to true makes the call asynchronous, enabling the user to return to interact with the page while the call processes in the background.

The status of the XHR request makes a number of calls to the onreadystatechange event handler. From within the event handler, you can check the status of the call by checking the readyState property on the XHR object: transport. The readyState property will store a number between 0 and 4 at any given time (see Table 5-1).

Table 5-1. *Possible* readyState *States*

Value	State	Description
0	Uninitialized	The open method of the XHR object hasn't been called yet.
1	Loading	The send method hasn't been called yet.
2	Loaded	The send method has been called; response headers are available.
3	Interactive	The response data is in the process of downloading, and is available via the responseText property of the XHR object.
4	Completed	Everything is done, and the entire result is available in the responseText and, if available, the responseXML properties of the XHR object.

It is standard practice to check for a readyState of 4 (it is the XHR equivalent of window.onload):

```
transport.onreadystatechange = function(){
  if(transport.readyState == 4)
  {
    alert('I am done!');
  }
};
```

That's all there is to it. Okay, not really. There is much more to consider, starting with the request/response process.

Ajax Request/Response Process

In a traditional request, a user initiates a request for data, waits for the server to send back a response, and then waits for the browser to render the page. In an Ajax-enabled environment, the amount of data that needs to be sent back and forth can be greatly reduced. Requests for data can also be made while the user is in the midst of completing another task on the page, negating the need for the user to initiate the request and wait for the entire response sequence to re-create the page. Responses need to return changes only to the current document, not the entire page (and any noncached assets such as images or CSS). You can then use JavaScript to update the document object model (DOM) without the page refresh.

Figure 5-3 illustrates the difference between Ajax and non-Ajax sequences. Ajax can ultimately mean a more responsive interface, taking less time to complete the same tasks.

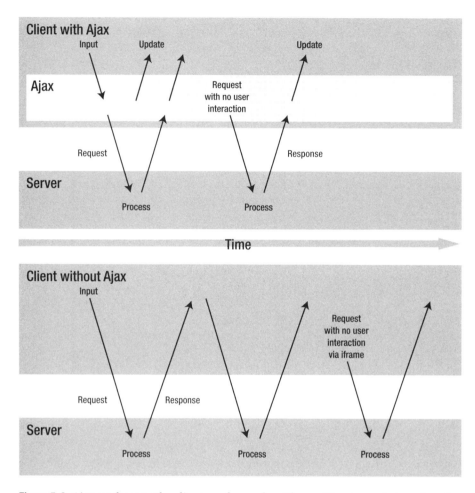

Figure 5-3. *Ajax updates to the client can be made with or without user interaction (in comparison with the traditional non-Ajax interaction).*

When putting together any Ajax-based solution, it's important to consider the user. Any time you override the default behavior of the browser there will suddenly be a number of points of failure. If something dies or takes too long to process, the user might never know what happened and might think that the site is broken.

If the request is user-initiated, it's important to show users that something is happening. This is most often done with an animated graphic indicator (see Figure 5-4) placed on or near where the interaction was initiated. The user then knows to wait or move onto some other part of the page to wait for the interaction to complete.

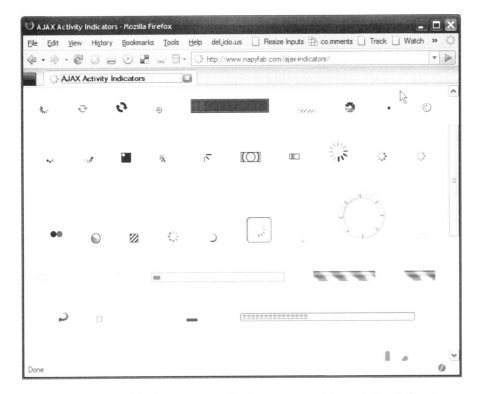

Figure 5-4. *A variety of the indicators available at* www.napyfab.com/ajax-indicators

Failure

As much as you might not like to admit it, sometimes things go wrong. So it's best to plan for it right from the get-go. Ask these questions:

- What happens if the request times out? How long should you wait?

- What happens when the data you get back isn't what was expected?

- What happens when multiple requests are made? (Especially if they come back in a different order from what was requested!)

You'll take a look at each of these questions and integrate solutions into a reusable library.

Storyboarding

When planning an Ajax-driven application, there are a number of interaction points. Yahoo! refers to them as *interesting moments*. Figure 5-5 shows a portion of the storyboard matrix that Yahoo! provides specifically for drag-and-drop functionality. I recommend that you have something similar to plan for the interesting moments in your application.

Figure 5-5. *Yahoo! storyboard matrix available at* `http://developer.yahoo.com/yui/dragdrop/` `#storyboard`

The Yahoo! implementation uses a grid with objects on the left and events along the top. Alternatively, I like to develop a flowchart that demonstrates the interactions that I might run into. In doing so, I can ensure that I build the various functions that might be required to handle the various issues. It also helps me think through the entire process instead of thinking strictly of the end goal.

Figure 5-6 is a sample flowchart that shows what might be involved in updating the data within an HTML table on the page. You'll notice that expired user sessions—a common problem in an authenticated application—have even been taken into account.

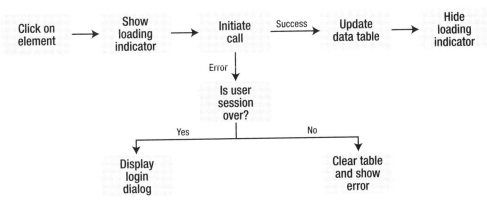

Figure 5-6. *A flowchart explaining the interaction process that might exist to update a data table*

With an understanding of the planning involved in implementing an Ajax-enabled inter-face, you'll now get an explanation of the different ways data can be exchanged. After that, you'll dive into actually building the Ajax object and planning for all of these scenarios.

Data Formats in Ajax

When you begin to look at data exchanges between the server and client with Ajax, you need to understand the different data formats that can be used to exchange data. You have access to two properties when an Ajax call returns to retrieve the data sent back from the server: `responseText` and `responseXML`. With `responseXML`, you have an XML object automatically ready to go. With `responseText`, you have to parse it into whatever format you think you need.

Note The `responseXML` property will be populated only if the server returns a valid XML document with the MIME type `text/xml`.

XML

The XHR object was made for returning XML results. It has a `responseXML` property in which XML is automatically parsed into a navigable object. You can then use familiar DOM methods to navigate it:

```
var doc = transport.responseXML.documentElement; // grabs the root node
var songs = doc.getElementsByTagName('song'); // get all song nodes
for(var i=0;i<songs.length;i++)
{
   // assuming each node just has text contained within it, we grab the
   // text node and display its contents.
   alert('I love ' + songs[i].firstChild.data);
}
```

Using the DOM in XML is a little different from using the DOM in HTML because you lose some of the conveniences, forcing you to get at data in a slightly different way. The previous example demonstrates this: in XML, text content is a node unto itself, just as it is in HTML, and must be retrieved using `firstChild` (because the text is the first and only child of the ele-ment). Then you use the `data` property of the text node to retrieve that text. You can also use the `nodeValue` property, which behaves the same way.

Let's take a look at some example XML and how you can use DOM methods to traverse that data and insert it into the page. In this example, you convert an XML document into a number of HTML elements:

```
<root>
  <book id="id15669">
    <title>The Long Road</title>
    <author>Hayden Smith</author>
    <description>Smith details his battles from the mailroom ...</description>
  </book>
  <book id="id15670">
    <title>Time: fact or fiction</title>
    <author>Dr. Michelle Doe</author>
    <description>Is time just a figment of our imagination?...</description>
  </book>
</root>
```

Here's the base structure of the HTML page that includes how you want to style each of the elements after you get them into the page. The book list will be inserted into the element with the ID of books:

```
<!DOCTYPE HTML PUBLIC "-//W3C//DTD HTML 4.01//EN"
  "http://www.w3.org/TR/html4/strict.dtd">
<html lang="en">
<head>
<title>Books</title>

<style type="text/css">
body {
  font-family:Arial,Helvetica,sans-serif;
  }
.book {
  border-top:1px solid #CCC;
  padding:10px 5px
  }
.book h2 {
  margin:0;
  font-size:1em;
  }
.book .author {
  margin:0;
  font-weight:bold;
  font-size:.9em;
  }
.book p {
  margin:0
  }
</style>
```

```
</head>
<body>
  <div id="books"></div>
</body>
</html>
```

The goal is to loop through each item and end up with the following HTML structure:

```
<div class="book" id="id15669">
  <h2>The Long Road</h2>
  <p class="author">Jonah Smith</p>
  <p>Smith details his battles from the mailroom to the CEO of Megacorp</p>
</div>
```

Within the response of the Ajax call, use getElementsByTagName() to retrieve all the book elements, looping through each one to add to the page. Using DOM methods, each of the elements and text nodes has to be created and appended to other nodes until finally the entire book branch can be appended into the books element:

```
var doc =  transport.responseXML.documentElement; // grabs the root node

var books = doc.getElementsByTagName('book'); // get all song nodes

var container = document.getElementById('books');
var book, title, author, description, text;
for(var i=0;i<books.length;i++)
{
  // create the book container
  book = document.createElement('div');
  book.className = 'book';
  book.id = books[i].getAttribute('id');

  // create the title
  title = document.createElement('h2');
  text = document.createTextNode(books[i].childNodes[1].firstChild.data);
  title.appendChild(text);
  book.appendChild(title);

  // create the author line
  author = document.createElement('p');
  author.className = 'author';
  text = document.createTextNode(books[i].childNodes[3].firstChild.data);
  author.appendChild(text);
  book.appendChild(author);
```

```
// create the description
description = document.createElement('p');
text = document.createTextNode(books[i].childNodes[5].firstChild.data);
description.appendChild(text);
book.appendChild(description);

// add the entire book node to the document
container.appendChild(book);
}
```

The code retrieves the first, third, and fifth elements. Remember that empty text nodes are considered elements, too, so you have to skip over them. The nice thing is that this behavior is consistent in all browsers *including* IE. The firstChild of the element is the text node and then the data property retrieves the text contained within. This should create an output that looks like Figure 5-7.

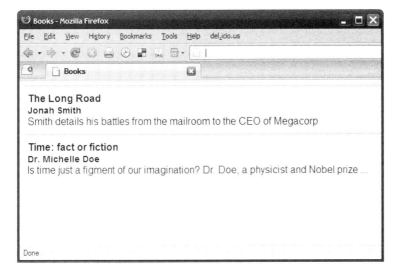

Figure 5-7. *The final output after converting the XML document into HTML*

Using DOM methods in this fashion can be very verbose. An alternative response to an Ajax call is to return the entire HTML structure within an XML node. However, before getting into that, it's extremely important that you understand how XML syntax works and behaves—especially with validity and encoding.

XML Validity and Encoding

XML is meant to be a very rigid language. No mistakes are allowed (it's affectionately known as "Draconian error handling"). This is a good thing for the most part, but it can catch you if you haven't considered a particular scenario of how it will be used. Take a look at the following two examples and see whether you can see the problem:

```
<myhtml>This is some content I want embedded on the page</myhtml>
<myhtml>This is some <strong>content</strong> I want embedded on the page</myhtml>
```

Now, if you were using the preceding syntax to embed this onto the page, it might look something like this:

```
var doc = transport.responseXML.documentElement; // grabs the root node
// get all myhtml nodes of which I have one
var embedhtml = doc.getElementsByTagName('myhtml')[1];
// Grab the element on the page in which to embed the html
var el = document.getElementById('placeholder');
el.innerHTML = embedhtml.firstChild.data;
```

With the first `<myhtml>` element, everything looks the way it should, and the entire string is embedded. But wait a second, from the second XML node example, only `"This is some"` appears on the page. That's because the `<strong>` tags are treated like another node, as shown in Figure 5-8.

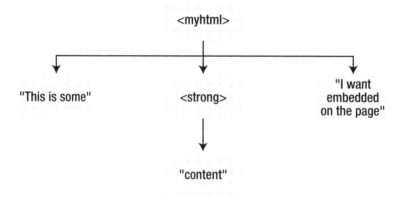

Figure 5-8. *What the XML structure looks like*

There are a couple of ways to get around having to parse through all the nodes: simply encode any HTML or embed the HTML in a CDATA node.

Encoding HTML

XML has five characters that can be encoded: &, <, >, ', and ". These characters can be encoded with their numerical character references or their predefined entities, as shown in Table 5-2.

Table 5-2. *Available Predefined Entities*

Character	Numerical Character Reference	Predefined Entity
&	&#38;	&amp;
<	&#60;	&lt;
>	&#62;	&gt;
'	&#39;	&apos;
"	&#34;	&quot;

Knowing this, you can re-encode the example from before:

```
<myhtml>This is some &lt;strong&gt;content&lt;/strong&gt;
    I want embedded on the page</myhtml>
```

If you are familiar with encoding characters in HTML, you can easily fall into another trap: using HTML entities in XML. This, too, will get caught by the XML error handling and fail.

```
<myhtml>This page copyright by Smith & Smith</myhtml>
<myhtml>This page copyright by Smith &amp; Smith</myhtml>
<myhtml>&copy; Smith &amp; Smith</myhtml>
```

The first example should be obvious because the ampersand hasn't been encoded. No problem in the second line because you've now properly encoded the ampersand. But in the final example, you're trying to use the HTML entity for the copyright symbol (©), which ultimately fails in the XML example. To fix it, simply encode the ampersand in the entity itself:

```
<myhtml>&amp;copy; Smith &amp; Smith</myhtml>
```

The ampersand entity gets turned into an ampersand upon retrieval and then the copyright entity gets converted into a copyright symbol upon insertion into the HTML DOM.

Let's take a look at the book example from before and see how you can approach it differently. The XML will need to contain the encoded HTML within each node:

```
<root>
  <book id="id15669">
    &lt;h2&gt;The Long Road&lt;/h2&gt;
    &lt;p class=&quot;author&quot;&gt;Jonah Smith&lt;/p&gt;
    &lt;p&gt;Smith details his battles from the mailroom to the CEO of Megacorp&lt;➡
/p&gt;
  </book>
  <book id="id15670">
    &lt;h2&gt;Time: fact or fiction&lt;/h2&gt;
    &lt;p class=&quot;author&quot;&gt;Dr. Michelle Doe&lt;/b&gt;&lt;/p&gt;
    &lt;p&gt;Is time just a figment of our imagination? Dr. Doe, a physicist and➡
 Nobel prize ...&lt;/p&gt;
  </book>
</root>
```

When you loop through, you can now simplify things greatly:

```
for(var i=0;i<books.length;i++)
{
  // create the book container
  book = document.createElement('div');
  book.className = 'book';
  book.id = books[i].getAttribute('id');
  book.innerHTML = books[i].firstChild.data;

  // add the entire book node to the document
  container.appendChild(book);
}
```

The bolded code is where you assign the contents of each book node into the container. You can even super-simplify it by including the entire HTML snippet as an escaped block:

```
<root>
  &lt;div class=&quot;book&quot; id=&quot;id15669&quot;&gt;
    &lt;h2&gt;The Long Road&lt;/h2&gt;
    &lt;p class=&quot;author&quot;&gt;Jonah Smith&lt;/p&gt;
    &lt;p&gt;Smith details his battles from the mailroom to the CEO of Megacorp&lt;➡
/p&gt;
  &lt;/div&gt;
  &lt;div class=&quot;book&quot; id=&quot;id15670&quot;&gt;
    &lt;h2&gt;Time: fact or fiction&lt;/h2&gt;
    &lt;p class=&quot;author&quot;&gt;Dr. Michelle Doe&lt;/b&gt;&lt;/p&gt;
    &lt;p&gt;Is time just a figment of our imagination? Dr. Doe, a physicist and➡
 Nobel prize ...&lt;/p&gt;
  &lt;/div&gt;
</root>
```

This way, you no longer have to loop through any elements; you can just append the contents directly into the container:

```
var doc =  transport.responseXML.documentElement; // grabs the root node
var books = doc.getElementsByTagName('book'); // get all song nodes
var container = document.getElementById('books');
container.innerHTML = doc.firstChild.data;
```

Escaping all that HTML, however, can make things hard to read and difficult to recognize that the HTML being returned is actually valid.

CDATA Nodes

The alternative to text nodes is CDATA sections. The World Wide Web Consortium (W3C) specification (http://www.w3.org/TR/2004/REC-xml-20040204/#sec-cdata-sect) describes them really well:

CDATA sections MAY *occur anywhere character data might occur; they are used to escape blocks of text containing characters which would otherwise be recognized as markup. CDATA sections begin with the string* "<![CDATA[" *and end with the string* "]]>".

CDATA sections give you a lot of flexibility and can remove much of the worry about encoding, which makes it easier to work with HTML content:

```
<myhtml><![CDATA[&copy; <strong>Smith &amp; Smith</strong>]]></myhtml>
```

Retrieving the content from a CDATA section works exactly like retrieving it from a text node. The book example would get encoded as follows:

```
<root><![CDATA[
  <div class="book" id="id15669">
    <h2>The Long Road</h2>
    <p class="author">Jonah Smith</p>
    <p>Smith details his battles from the mailroom to the CEO of Megacorp</p>
  </div>
  <div class="book" id="id15670">
    <h2>Time: fact or fiction</h2>
    <p class="author">Dr. Michelle Doe</b></p>
    <p>Is time just a figment of our imagination? Dr. Doe, a physicist and➡
 Nobel prize ...</p>
  </div>
]]></root>
```

Already, the HTML is much easier to understand. Embedding that entire snippet is handled exactly the same as it was before:

```
var doc =  transport.responseXML.documentElement; // grabs the root node
var books = doc.getElementsByTagName('book'); // get all song nodes
var container = document.getElementById('books');
container.innerHTML = doc.firstChild.data;
```

XSLT

One reason to use XML as a data format is to take advantage of XSLT, which is a transformation language that converts an XML document into another format (most often another XML format such as XHTML). Unfortunately, cross-browser support is often slow or buggy with libraries built to address these shortcomings:

- **Google AJAXSLT** (http://goog-ajaxslt.sourceforge.net/): Google released its cross-browser XSLT library as open source and it includes support for Safari 1.3+, Opera 7.5+, IE 6+, and Firefox 1+.

- **Sarissa** (http://dev.abiss.gr/sarissa/): Sarissa acts as a cross-browser wrapper for a number of XML application programming interfaces (APIs), including XMLDocument, XMLElement, XMLHttpRequest, XMLSerializer, and XSLTProcessor.

Because client-side XSLT is almost always intended to convert an XML document into HTML, I recommend that you avoid the hassle of dealing with cross-browser issues and create the HTML snippet on the server side.

Alternatives to XML

As handy as XML might seem to be, it's not without its downsides. It can be a complicated method of navigating the document and it is verbose. Also, having to deal with a variety of cross-browser issues is never fun. So, you can turn to `responseText` and discover some other possibilities. A string response can be quite powerful because you can transform that string into something much more useful.

HTML

This is super sweet and easy. All you have to do is return an HTML snippet and then insert that snippet into the document:

```
var htmlSnippet = transport.responseText; // grabs the text response
var el = document.getElementById('placeholder');
el.innerHTML = htmlSnippet;
```

Note If you return an HTML snippet with a `<script>` element embedded within it, the code will not execute.

JavaScript

If you have conditional JavaScript that you want to execute but not cache as you normally would, you can return the code via the `responseText` and then `eval()` it:

```
eval(transport.responseText); // grabs the text response
```

This technique isn't one I've used often. Including the JavaScript with the `<script>` element in the `<head>` is still the most practical approach. However, there is a variation to this technique that has gained much popularity, possibly even surpassing XML as the preferred approach for data transfer: JavaScript Object Notation (JSON).

JSON has been growing in popularity because of its XML-like structure and its capability to integrate well into a JavaScript-based application (because it *is* JavaScript).

JSON syntax is a subset of object notation and is designed to make it more readily interchangeable with other programming languages. A JSON object is an object literal that contains only the following types: strings, numbers, arrays, or other object literals. Strings should use double quotes (JSON also requires that the keys be in double quotes).

The following is a JSON object showing the contents of a shopping cart. It contains two object literals, `fruits` and `vegetables`, each containing a number of items:

```
var shoppingCart = {
    "fruits": {
        "apples":5,
        "apricots":4,
        "oranges":6,
        "mangos":5
    },
    "vegetables":{
        "celery":2,
        "lettuce":1,
        "green peppers":5
    }
};
```

To reference the `celery` element:

```
shoppingCart.vegetables.celery; //  or...
shoppingCart["vegetables"]["celery"];
```

You'll notice that `"green peppers"` has a space in it. Because it is a string, the space is perfectly valid. However, when using spaces for member names, just remember that you can't use dot notation to refer to them. Therefore, you have to refer to the property `"green peppers"` using bracket notation:

```
shoppingCart.vegetables["green peppers"]; // or...
shoppingCart["vegetables"]["green peppers"];
```

Parsers are available for languages such as .NET, PHP, and Java that recognize and can convert JSON into native objects for those languages. You can find more information on JSON at the JSON web site: `http://www.json.org`.

Note Strings should be enclosed in double quotes ("), not just single quotes ('). While the single quotes will work when evaluating the code in JavaScript, any attempts to parse the JSON object using a JSON parser (server side or client side) will likely result in an error.

When JSON data is returned from the server, it needs to be evaluated just like any other data. Because of the potential for code injection attacks (never assume that the data you receive is safe), I highly recommend using a client-side parser such as the one on the JSON web site.

```
var obj = transport.responseText.parseJSON();
if(obj) performMagic(obj);
```

You would then check that the data you were expecting exists and then move on to process the data accordingly.

Delimited Strings

A *delimited string* is one that separates values with a character. For example, a query string of a URL is separated by ampersands, and key/value pairs are separated by an equal sign:

```
search=my+search+phrase&sortBy=title&page=2
```

Converting a query string into a JavaScript object requires two passes to build up the object. The first pass splits the string at the ampersand, and the second pass separates the key/value pairs:

```
var qs = "search=my+search+phrase&sortBy=title&page=2";
var data = qs.split('&');
for(var i=0;i<data.length;i++)
{
   data[i] = data[i].split('=');
}
alert(data[1][1]); // alerts "title"
```

By the end, you'd have a multidimensional array. To access a key/value pair, you'd have to know where in the array the value exists or else loop through all the items in the first dimension of the array to find what you're looking for. Alternatively, you might want to turn the key/value pairs into an object, making it easier to access the parameters:

```
var qsObject = {}; // our object store
var qs = "search=my+search+phrase&sortBy=title&page=2";
var data = qs.split('&');
var tmp;
for(var i=0;i<data.length;i++)
{
   tmp = data[i].split('=');
   qsObject[tmp[0]] = tmp[1];
}
alert(qsObject.sortBy); // alerts "title"
```

Keep in mind that if there are duplicate keys, the last one defined in the query string will take precedence.

You can use a comma-separated value (CSV) as another format for separating a string into a number of parts. Each record is separated by a new line, and each field is separated by a comma (hence *comma-separated*). Parsing a line of CSV isn't just a matter of splitting the string at the commas. Take a look at this example:

```
"Mr. Smith, Esq.", 2006, January, 26,Need to get in touch
```

Notice the comma in the first field. The entire field gets wrapped in quotes to indicate that it's all one field. And what if you have quotes inside a field? It gets even more complicated. What if you have empty records? Yup, even more difficult. String parsing in this fashion is practical only with simple data sets that are easily separated.

Returning the data in any other format besides JSON usually means parsing the data into JavaScript before you can manipulate it; hence the reason JSON has become such a popular format.

■**Caution** As much as you want to think the data coming back to you is reliable, it might not be. Be suspicious of anything and plan for it accordingly.

Building a Reusable Ajax Object

Now that you have an understanding of Ajax and how its information can be sent back and forth, let's look at creating an object that you can use with the projects.

The first thing you need to do is create an object that you can instantiate. You'll want to make it a reusable class because you'll need to instantiate the object with each request you want to make:

```
function Ajax()
{
  var transport;
  if(window.XMLHttpRequest) {
    transport = new XMLHttpRequest();
  }else{
    try{ transport = new ActiveXObject("MSXML2.XMLHTTP.6.0");  }catch(e){}
    try{ transport = new ActiveXObject("MSXML2.XMLHTTP");  }catch(e){}
  }
  if(!transport) return;
  this.transport = transport;
}

Ajax.prototype.send = function(url, options)
{
  if(!this.transport) return;
  var transport = this.transport;
  var _options = {
      method:"GET",
      callback:function(){}
      };

  // override options
   for(var key in options)
   {
     _options[key] = options[key];
   }

   transport.open(_options.method, url, true);
   transport.onreadystatechange = function(){ _options.callback(transport) };
   transport.send();
}
```

In the object constructor, you establish which object you can use. First, you test for the existence of the XMLHttpRequest object, which is supported in all modern browsers, including Firefox 1+, Safari 1.2+, Opera 7.6+, and IE 7+. For IE 5 and 6 (or IE 7 users who might have the native object turned off), try to instantiate the ActiveX versions of the XHR object.

You try to instantiate them in try/catch blocks because IE will generate an alert dialog if the ActiveX objects are turned off altogether. First, test for the most recent version of the XHR object; if that fails, try to use a fallback version. (See the section "What Do All the Different ActiveX Objects Mean?" for more information.)

With the constructor complete, you need to give the object a send() method so that you can actually send requests to the server. I've set it up to take two parameters: the URL that you want to request and then an options object.

Note Remember that passing in optional parameters using an object literal is a great way to keep the code clear and concise.

Right now, there are only two optional properties: method (GET or POST) and callback. The callback property gets called every time the readyState of the Ajax object changes. Once the options are mapped to the internal _options object, open the URL, attach the event handler, and then send the request.

Note If you want to reuse this Ajax object to send another request, the onreadystatechange event has to be declared after the open call; otherwise IE 5 or 6 will fail on every call after the first.

Now, let's take a look at how to use the fancy new Ajax object:

```
function processRequest(transport)
{
  if(transport.readyState == 4)
  {
    var obj = transport.responseText.parseJSON();
  }
}
```

You set up the callback function, which takes the transport as its one and only parameter. Within the callback function, see whether the state is equal to 4, which indicates that the object has properly returned a result. In this case, you're using the JSON library to parse the response and turn it into a JavaScript object.

With all the pieces in place, it's time to send out the request:

```
var ajax = new Ajax();
ajax.send('/path/to/script', {callback:processRequest});
```

I specified the URL that I want to call and specified the callback option, assigning to it the processRequest() function. I didn't specify the method because it automatically defaults to GET.

What Do All the Different ActiveX Objects Mean?

If you've scoured through any number of Ajax solutions, you might have noticed different XMLHttpRequest objects being referred to. Microsoft's XML implementation, which is known as MSXML, comes in many versions.

Here's the list:

- Microsoft.XMLHTTP

- Msxml2.XMLHTTP

- Msxml2.XMLHTTP.3.0

- Msxml2.XMLHTTP.4.0

- Msxml2.XMLHTTP.5.0

- Msxml2.XMLHTTP.6.0

An article from the Microsoft XML team explains in some detail the differences between the different versions and how they should be used (but it's still not entirely clear: http://blogs.msdn.com/xmlteam/archive/2006/10/23/using-the-right-version-of-msxml-in-internet-explorer.aspx).

MSXML 1.0 and 2.0 are no longer supported by Microsoft. Version 4.0 never saw an operating system release, and version 5.0 was a special version for Microsoft Office. The version-independent IDs, Microsoft.XMLHTTP and Msxml2.XMLHTTP, now map directly to version 3.0 (even if version 6.0 is installed). This really only leaves you with two possible program IDs (referred to as progIDs by Microsoft):

- Msxml2.XMLHTTP

- Msxml2.XMLHTTP.6.0

Version 6 was introduced in IE 7 and includes some bug fixes (such as the one mentioned earlier, in which IE 5 and 6 fail when the onreadystatechange is declared before the open call). Although IE 7 includes a native XHR object, users have the option of disabling it. Therefore, it's a good idea to test for Msxml2.XMLHTTP.6.0 first; if it doesn't work, fall back to the other version.

Planning for Failure

Now that you have the basic Ajax object in place, let's review possible problems and work to build solutions to those problems into the object:

- What happens if the request times out? How long should you wait?

- What happens when the data you get back isn't what was expected?

- What happens when multiple requests are made? (Especially if they come back in a different order from what was requested!)

Handling Timeouts

Ajax calls usually stay open for as long as the server keeps the connection open. However, if you have an unresponsive server, it might be too long for the user to wait. A more ideal solution is to simply time out the call and handle the error. I made the necessary updates to the Ajax object, which I highlighted in bold:

```
function Ajax()
{
  var transport;
  if(window.XMLHttpRequest) {
    transport = new XMLHttpRequest();
  }else{
    try{ transport = new ActiveXObject("MSXML2.XMLHTTP.6.0");  }catch(e){}
    try{ transport = new ActiveXObject("MSXML2.XMLHTTP");  }catch(e){}
  }
  if(!transport) return;
  this.transport = transport;
}

Ajax.prototype.send = function(url, options)
{
  if(!this.transport) return;
  var transport = this.transport;
  var aborted = false;
  var _options = {
      method:"GET",
      timeout:5,
      onerror:function(){},
      onsuccess:function(){}
      };

  // override options
   for(var key in options)
   {
     _options[key] = options[key];
   }

   function checkForTimeout()
   {
     if(transport.readyState != 4)
     {
       aborted = true;
       transport.abort();
     }
   }
   setTimeout(checkForTimeout, _options.timeout * 1000);
```

```
function onreadystateCallback()
{
 if(transport.readyState == 4)
 {
    if( !aborted && transport.status >= 200 && transport.status < 300 )
    {
      _options.onsuccess(transport);
    }else{
      _options.onerror(transport);
    }
  }
}

transport.open(_options.method, url, true);
transport.onreadystatechange = onreadystateCallback;
transport.send('');
}
```

A bunch of new stuff has been added here, so let's go through things one chunk at a time:

```
var aborted = false;
var _options = {
    method:"GET",
    timeout:5,
    onerror:function(){},
    onsuccess:function(){}
    };
```

The aborted variable is a flag you'll use to determine later whether you had to abort the call manually. The _options object gets a timeout variable, which defines how many seconds you should wait before giving up on the request. The _options object also loses its callback property that gets replaced with onerror() and onsuccess() functions.

```
function checkForTimeout()
{
    if(transport.readyState != 4)
    {
      aborted = true;
      transport.abort();
    }
}
setTimeout(checkForTimeout, _options.timeout * 1000);
```

A function is set up, which you'll call after the timeout period to see whether the object has successfully returned. If it hasn't, set the aborted variable to true to indicate that you manually had to end this call; you use the abort method on the XHR object. Doing so will automatically execute the onreadystatechange event handler.

```
function onreadystateCallback()
{
 if(transport.readyState == 4)
 {
    if( !aborted && transport.status >= 200 && transport.status < 300 )
    {
      _options.onsuccess(transport);
    }else{
      _options.onerror(transport);
    }
 }
}
```

```
transport.open(_options.method, url, true);
transport.onreadystatechange = onreadystateCallback;
transport.send();
```

The `onreadystateCallback()` function handles the `onreadystatechange` event. Within the `onreadystateCallback()` function, check the status and dispatch to either the `onsuccess` or the `onerror` event handlers accordingly. I check to see whether the call was aborted manually and then whether the HTTP status code is between 200 and 300, which indicates a successful call. The HTTP status code is accessed via the `status` attribute of the XHR object.

Finally, the `onreadystatechange` event handler was changed from the one that you had originally passed in via the options object to the internal handler.

HTTP Status Codes

Whenever a browser makes a call, the server sends back a response. Within the response, a status code is returned, letting the browser know some vital information. For an in-depth view of all the possible status codes, check out the HTTP/1.1 recommendation from the W3C (`www.w3.org/Protocols/rfc2616/rfc2616-sec10.html`).

What you hope to see is a status of 200, which indicates a successful response. Anything within the 200 range is a success. A response in the 300 range is a redirection. The browser will automatically handle the redirection and retrieve the new document, which should then return the 200 response status. The 400 range is considered a client error. The request might not have been sent correctly, or you asked for a page that doesn't exist—that is, the dreaded 404! Last but not least, the 500 range indicates a server error of some sort. When it comes to Ajax requests, you want a response only in the 200 range. The previous code examples already did this by checking that the status was greater than or equal to 200 and less than 300.

```
if( !aborted && transport.status >= 200 && transport.status < 300 )
```

Multiple Requests

It's very likely that after you build an Ajax-enabled web site or application, you'll need to make multiple requests. There are two different scenarios with multiple requests that you have to plan for:

- An initial request is made, but then a subsequent call is made that should override the first call. For example, a user fills out a search box and then presses Enter. But before the call has returned, the user realizes that a mistake was made, corrects it, and presses Enter again. The user doesn't want the first set of results—only the second. You'll need to detect that a second request has been made and determine whether you need to override the original request.

- The other scenario is when you make sequential calls, but the calls return out of order. For example, you have a chat program that continually polls the server for new messages. Messages need to be returned in the same order.

If you need to keep your calls in order, essentially mimicking a synchronous system with an asynchronous one, you need to keep track of each call through a token. The token could just be an integer that you increment each time you make a call.

Then you process the callbacks only when the current token is the next valid token; or if a record or two is skipped, wait until the missing record comes in or times out.

Unexpected Data

You should never assume what data comes back from the server. You've already got an onerror handler in case the server throws back something unusual. Beyond that, though, you should add an extra level of error checking.

If you are expecting your data back in a particular format, such as XML or JSON, include a server-based contingency plan that populates the return with an error code of some kind. Then check for the error code on the client side before processing your results. If the server doesn't return what you want (for example, it returns an invalid JSON object or an unhandled server-side error), you'll need to handle that on the client side as well.

Here is a JSON example:

```
{"error":{"id":1,"message":"Your session has expired"}}
```

In the onsuccess event handler that you attached, you would have the following code:

```
var UNKNOWN = 0;
function processRequestSuccess(transport)
{
  var obj = transport.responseText.parseJSON();
  // if JSON parsing didn't work then no object exists
  // which means the server failed somehow
  if(!obj)
  {
    processError(UNKNOWN);
    return;
  }
  // if I have an error property in my object, the server
  // returned an error message and failed gracefully.
  if(obj.error)
  {
    processError(obj.error.id, obj.error.message);
  }
```

```
  // continue to process request normally
  // ...
}
```

The `processError()` function would simply take the parameters and process the error. It could display an alert dialog or it could write the error message to the page.

Using Libraries to Handle Ajax Calls

As you've seen, there is a lot to consider each time an Ajax call is made. Many of the JavaScript libraries mentioned in the previous chapter include an Ajax component. This is a perfect example of why JavaScript libraries are so popular: most of the hard work is already done for you. With a larger user base, bugs are found more quickly, and many of the planning issues are already thought out for you. Let's step through a few examples using various libraries.

Prototype

The Prototype library has some very handy Ajax functionality built in:

```
new Ajax.Request(url, {
  method: 'get',
  onSuccess: function(transport) {  }
});
```

The format that the Prototype library takes is actually quite similar to the way you approached the object. They go much farther in automating a number of features, however. For example, there are event handlers for more than just success or failure. You can hook into a number of events, such as the following:

- `onCreate`: Is used after the object is instantiated but before any of the methods of the object are used.

- `onComplete`: Fires upon completion of the request and after the other event handlers have been fired. This is a good place to stop any animation or loading indicator you might be using.

- `onException`: Fires if it could not process the request. For example, if there was an improperly formatted JSON object returned, this event would fire.

- `onFailure`: Fires if the call ends and there is no valid HTTP status code between 200 and 300 (similar to the way the custom object you saw earlier worked).

- `onSuccess`: Behaves just like the object and fires when the call has successfully completed.

- `onXXX`: Where X is the HTTP status code; unlikely to be something you'd use very often because 200 is the most common return.

Some nice features of Prototype include its automatic handling of JSON. If the content-type returned from the server is `text/javascript` or `application/javascript` (or a few other variations), the `responseText` will automatically get parsed by its JSON filter. Alternatively, you can pass data in on the X-JSON header but the amount of data you could pass in through that is limited (this would be a reasonable place to put JSON-based error messaging, as covered earlier).

Ajax.Updater

Ajax.Updater, which is a specialization of the Ajax.Request object, takes responseText and automatically inserts it into the HTML element of your choosing:

```
new Ajax.Updater(container, url, options)
```

The options parameter is exactly the same as before, except with a couple of additional options, most notably the insertion property. By default, the Updater replaces the content within the element. However, the contents can be appended to what is already there with the insertion parameter. The insertion parameter takes an Insertion object (another Prototype class) that enables you to specify whether the contents come before the element (Insertion.Before), at the top of the element (Insertion.Top), at the bottom of the element (Insertion.Bottom), or after the element (Insertion.After).

To build a really simple chat program, there is a chat window, a text box, and a send button:

```
<div id="chat"></div>
<input type="text" id="msg" value="test">
<input type="button" id="send" value="Send">
```

To hook up the send button, add an event observer to it, sending the contents of the msg input to the server. When the Ajax call returns, it automatically places the response at the end of the chat element.

```
function sendMessage()
{
  // update the chat element with the response
  new Ajax.Updater($('chat'), '/path/to/script', {
    parameters: { text: $('msg') },
    insertion: Insertion.Bottom
  });
}
// run sendMessage any time the send button is clicked
Event.observe($('send'), 'click', sendMessage);
```

Ajax.PeriodicalUpdater

If you want to add server polling to the chat program, you can extend the application with the PeriodicalUpdater. As you can likely surmise, the PeriodicalUpdater will make a call to the server every *X* seconds and update the chat element with the response:

```
new Ajax.PeriodicalUpdater($('chat'), '/path/to/script', {
  frequency: 2, /* 2 seconds */
  insertion: Insertion.Bottom
});
```

YUI

With the YUI library, everything is handled through the connection manager. Here's an example:

```
var transaction = YAHOO.util.Connect.asyncRequest('GET', sUrl, callback);
```

The first parameter tells YUI whether you are making a GET or POST request. The second parameter is the URL to request. The third parameter is a callback object. The object stores the success and failure callback functions as well as enabling you to pass arguments into the call to be available upon return.

```
var callback = {
  success: myObject.processRequestSuccess,
  failure: myObject.processRequestFailure,
  argument: [argument1, argument2, argument3],
  scope: myObject
}
```

You can also specify the scope that should be passed to the function calls. That way, if the success and failure callbacks are part of a larger object, you can maintain the scope for the this variable.

If performing a POST request, you can pass the data in with a query string format as a fourth parameter:

```
var transaction = YAHOO.util.Connect.asyncRequest('POST', sUrl, callback,➡
 'key1=encoded+data&key2=even+more+data');
```

The YUI library even has a nice function to take all form fields and automatically append them into a request (removing the need to specify the fourth parameter):

```
YAHOO.util.Connect.setForm(formObject);
var conn = YAHOO.util.Connect.asyncRequest('POST', 'http://example.com/', callback);
```

jQuery

jQuery is heavily designed around manipulating the DOM. Its Ajax approach takes the Prototype Ajax.Updater to another level:

```
$('#myelement').load('/updatestatus');
```

As you saw in the last chapter, the $ function grabs the elements (in this case, an element with an ID of myelement). With that, it requests the updatestatus URL and replaces the contents of the element with the response.

You can also make regular Ajax calls through the ajax() method of the jQuery object:

```
var options = {
    url: 'document.xml',
    type: 'GET',
    dataType: 'xml',
    timeout: 1000,
    error: function(){
        alert('Error loading XML document');
    },
    success: function(xml){
        // do something with xml
    }
}
$.ajax(options);
```

All options, including the URL, are sent through an object literal as the only parameter.

Summary

In this chapter you took a look at what Ajax is and what it means in comparison with traditional page calls. You took a look at the various data exchange formats available to you and which approach might be more appropriate for certain situations.

The chapter stepped through building a custom Ajax object. It then showed how to extend the object to plan for contingencies. Finally, the chapter took a look at how to take advantage of popular JavaScript libraries to handle the grunt work for you.

In Chapter 6, you'll take a look at visual effects and how they can be integrated into your sites.

CHAPTER 6

■ ■ ■

Visual Effects

From animations and slides to fades, visual effects can add some sex and sizzle to a page. While these effects can be easily overdone, you'll soon understand why you should add them to a page and what problems they solve. With that understanding, you'll build your own animation object to demonstrate the concepts you've learned so far. To cap it all off, you'll learn how to use the JavaScript libraries talked about in Chapter 4 to handle these animation effects.

Why Use Visual Effects?

Visual effects sometimes have a reputation for being flashy or even gaudy. In some cases they are, but animations can actually be quite helpful. Effects help to alert users or inform them that stuff is happening on the page.

Traditionally, any interaction with a web page exhibited predictable feedback. You clicked a link or a form submit button, and the browser icon would then begin rotating until the page refreshed and completed loading. In an Ajax-driven application in which page refreshes can disappear altogether, the user needs to be notified that certain actions have happened or are in the process of occurring.

For example, Google applications such as Mail and Calendar indicate that they are in the process of retrieving more data by using a loading indicator in the top-right corner of the page, as seen in Figure 6-1.

Indicators and animations let users know that they are still in charge and that something hasn't mysteriously broken.

Animations can also be put to good use when revealing or hiding information. Basic scripts often just toggle visibility, but if users aren't paying close attention, they might not be instantly aware of what just happened. Animate the element and the user will take notice and draw a direct correlation between the cause and the effect.

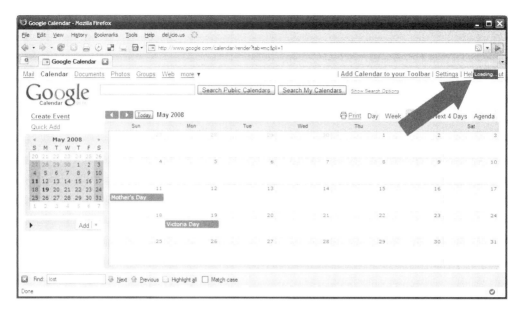

Figure 6-1. *The loading indicator in Google Calendar*

Animations can add to the experience in other ways, too:

• Drop-down menus that fade or slide aren't as jarring to the user as a sudden on/off switch, especially as the user slides over multiple navigation items.

• Links to named anchors (links that start with the number sign: #) can cause the browser to glide to the anchor instead of instantly displaying the section. For links to places elsewhere on the same page, users understand that they haven't been sent to another page; they are just in another location on the same page.

• In a drag and drop, animating the dragged item back to its original location when the user lets go of it can make clear to the user that the drop didn't happen.

It is prudent not to overdo animations, of course. In particular, it's important to keep animations short and snappy. Taking too long to complete an animation means that users are left waiting for the animation to complete before proceeding with the task they want to accomplish. Although most animations should probably be no more than half a second long, interact with what you're building and ensure that it feels snappy without going crazy.

Yahoo! has a Design Pattern Library that discusses various patterns and their uses in depth. Many of the patterns cover animations and transitions, the problems they solve, and the caveats that go along with them. You can check it out at http://developer.yahoo.com/ypatterns/index.php.

Building a Simple Animation Object

Now that you have a sense of why you might want to animate something, let's look at building your own animation object. Animating an element can be fairly simple: you take an element and then change one or more of its properties over time.

Because you'll want the possibility of animating multiple objects, you should make it a class construct. Define the function to take five parameters: the element to animate, the property you want to change, the start value, the end value, and the length of time it should take to complete the transition:

```
function Animation(element, property, from, to, duration){ }
```

The animation object would then be instantiated using the following structure:

```
new Animation('elementID', 'left', 0, 200, 1000);
```

When it comes to building any code, it's a good idea to think through the implementation. There are pros and cons to every decision taken, and you should always consider why you make each decision.

Taking a look at the code so far, you can see that the element ID is passed in as a string, presumably to retrieve the element within the animation object via the document object model (DOM) method `document.getElementById()` or with a JavaScript library call such as `$()`. If you use a library call, you inevitably tie the animation object to that library of choice. Alternately, you can stick with the DOM method, but it's a little verbose. In this case, though, you have to do it only once, so you should use the DOM method and keep things library agnostic. The call is assigned to a variable to make it easier to refer to the element throughout the object.

```
function Animation(element, property, from, to, duration)
{
  var el = document.getElementById(element);
  if(!el) return false;
}
```

A quick error check is performed to see whether the element exists, which can prevent unsightly errors from popping up in the user's browser because an element wasn't defined. You can then leave it up to the developer to fail from this error gracefully.

What if you want to perform an animation on an element that doesn't have an ID? To make this class even more flexible, let's expect an element reference to be passed in instead of just an ID string. Even better, check to see whether the element property passed in is an ID string. If it's a string and not an object reference, you'll retrieve the element by using the DOM method. The best of both worlds!

```
function Animation(element, property, from, to, duration)
{
  var el = element;
  if(typeof el == 'string') el = document.getElementById(element);
  if(!el) return false;
}
new Animation(document.getElementById('elementID'), 'left', 0, 200, 1000);
```

You have five parameters, but glancing at the code to instantiate an object gives you little insight about what the numbers mean. You have to refer to the class definition to understand what the values mean. To solve this problem, you can switch the parameters to an object literal to take advantage of named keys. This change also gives you the flexibility to expand the

application programming interface (API) without making the instantiation even more complicated. So change that around now by passing in only an options argument and pulling the
element ID from that options object:

```
function Animation(options)
{
  var el = options.element;
  if(typeof el == 'string') el = document.getElementById(options.element);
  if(!el) return false;
}
```

Now when you want to instantiate the object, you can simply pass in an options object:

```
var options = {
      element:document.getElementById('elementID'),
      property: 'left',
      from: 0,
      to: 200,
      duration: 1000
    };
  new Animation(options);
```

Next you need to perform the animation. Unfortunately, however, there's no way to just
tell the document to animate an item. Like traditional animation, you place the element in a
new location after a fraction of time, which is done with small changes at multiple times per
second. This process creates the illusion of movement, as demonstrated (as well as a static
image can) in Figure 6-2.

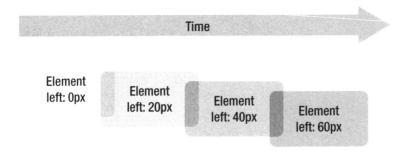

Figure 6-2. *Changing the value over time*

To do this, you need to use either setInterval() or setTimeout(). What's the difference?
Both take two parameters: the first is the code to execute, and the second is the amount of
time in milliseconds to wait before being called. Both return an ID that can be used to cancel
the call whenever you want:

```
var intervalID = setInterval(performAnimation, 1000); // call function every 1000 ms
var timeoutID = setTimeout(performAnimation, 1000); // call function in 1000 ms
```

You can also pass in a string to be evaluated, which can be handy to pass in variables (I prefer the previous approach, though):

```
var intervalID = setInterval("performAnimation("+id+")", 1000);
var timeoutID = setTimeout("performAnimation("+id+")", 1000);
```

The difference between `setInterval()` and `setTimeout()` is that `setTimeout()` will execute the code only once, whereas `setInterval()` will continue to execute the code every second (or whatever interval you set) until the call is cancelled.

To prevent `setInterval()` from firing, just call `clearInterval()` with the ID that was returned when you called the `setInterval()` function:

```
clearInterval(intervalID);
```

Likewise, to stop the `setTimeout()` call from firing, just call `clearTimeout()` with the ID that was returned from the `setTimeout()` function. Trying to clear a timeout after it has fired or with an invalid ID doesn't do anything, so you don't have to worry about JavaScript errors.

```
clearTimeout(timeoutID);
```

Now that you have two ways to approach the timed sequences, you have to consider how you want to approach the animation. On one hand, you can mimic the film approach by running so many times a second. The general minimum number of frames per second (fps) to avoid choppy animation is 24, but you'll usually see round numbers such as 30fps. Setting the frame rate is really easy to do with `setInterval()`:

```
var intervalID = setInterval(performAnimation, 33);
```

The first parameter is the function that you want to call, and the second parameter is 33 (1,000 milliseconds divided by 30fps and rounded to the nearest integer).

The other way you can calculate the frame rate is to look at the property that you want to change and determine how many steps (pixels [px]) it would take to animate it over a certain time frame. For example, if you have a property that you want to move from the left, starting at 50px and ending at 200px over a period of 3 seconds, calculate that at 200 minus 50 divided by 3 seconds = 50 iterations per second. Divide 1,000 milliseconds by 50 iterations, and you get the following:

```
var intervalID = setInterval(performAnimation, 20);
```

This formula might work well for small iterations, but if you have an object that needs to go from 0 to 1,000 in 1 second, that's 1,000 iterations, but only 30 are required to give the appearance of a smooth animation. Therefore, you should implement the first approach into the script:

```
function Animation(options)
{
  var el = options.element;
  if(typeof el == 'string') el = document.getElementById(options.element);
  if(!el) return false;
  var fps = 30;
```

```
    function animate()
    {
    }

    var intervalID = setInterval(animate, 1000 / fps);
}
```

You now have a timer running and executing at 30fps. Next up, you need to take the object that you want to animate and determine how many steps it will take to animate, given the current frame rate and duration. After that, it's simply a matter of incrementing the steps each time you run the animate() function. After you reach the number of steps, clear the interval—and the animation is done. This is the basic animation class:

```
function Animation(options)
{
  var el = options.element;
  if(typeof el == 'string') el = document.getElementById(options.element);
  if(!el) return false;
  var fps = 30;
  // stores which step we're on
  var step = 0;
  // determines the total number of steps
  var numsteps = options.duration / 1000 * fps;
  // determines the interval between each step
  var interval = (options.from - options.to) / numsteps;

  function animate()
  {
     // what the new position will be
     var newval = options.from - (step * interval);
     // the step increments AFTER the comparison
     if(step++ < numsteps) {
       // use Math.ceil to round to an integer and style
       el.style[options.property] =  Math.ceil(newval) + 'px';
     }else{
       // set the element to its final spot
       el.style[options.property] =  options.to + 'px';
       // clear the interval. the intervalID is available
       // via the closure
       clearInterval(intervalID);
     }
  }

  var intervalID = setInterval(animate, 1000 / fps);
}
```

This animation object can now modify a DOM property upon instantiation. But what if you want more control on the animation process (for example, being able to decide when to start, stop, or reset the animation)? Let's extend the object further with some new methods. You'll add `start()` and `stop()`, which will work like the play and stop buttons on a tape recorder (er, CD player—sorry, I mean MP3 player). However, while you're here, let's add a couple of extra methods: `gotoStart()` and `gotoEnd()`. Using the multimedia machine analogy, they will enable you to rewind or fast forward the animation, if need be.

There are two key changes that you need to make. The first is to have the `setInterval()` not run automatically on instantiation, but to have it only when you run `start()`. The other change is to offer up a public API by returning an object as a result of instantiation (this is a great example of the encapsulation that was covered in Chapter 3):

```
function Animation(options)
{
  var el = options.element;
  if(typeof el == 'string') el = document.getElementById(options.element);
  if(!el) return false;
  var fps = 30;
  // stores which step we're on
  var step = 0;
  // determines the total number of steps
  var numsteps = options.duration / 1000 * fps;
  // determines the interval between each step
  var interval = (options.from - options.to) / numsteps;
  var intervalID;

  function animate()
  {
    // what the new position will be
    var newval = options.from - (step * interval);
    // the step increments AFTER the comparison
    if(step++ < numsteps) {
      // use Math.ceil to round to an integer and style
      el.style[options.property] =  Math.ceil(newval) + 'px';
    }else{
      el.style[options.property] =  options.to + 'px';
      publicMethods.stop();
    }
  }

  var publicMethods = {
    start:function(){
      intervalID = setInterval(animate, 1000 / fps);
    },
    stop:function(){
      clearInterval(intervalID);
    },
```

```
    gotoStart:function(){
      step = 0;
      el.style[options.property] = options.from + 'px';
    },
    gotoEnd:function(){
      step = numsteps;
      el.style[options.property] = options.to + 'px';
    }
  }
  return publicMethods;
}
```

The `interval` variable was moved up to the top, so it's with the rest of the variables. The declaration is not moved to the `start()` function because you still need closures to be able to access that variable in the `stop()` method. The other thing you'll notice is that the `animate()` function now runs the `stop()` method instead of just clearing the interval. This keeps all "stop" logic in one place, which will be important as you continue to extend the API.

How can you possibly extend the API? Read on.

Callbacks

After you have the animation object all set to animate in an agnostic way, you might want to create custom events that fire at certain times, enabling other code to tie into the animation to perform related tasks. In any animation, there are usually only three interesting moments:

- **The start of the animation:** Tying into the start of an animation can be helpful if something you want to do is tied into the start of a particular animation. For example, you might have a text label that needs to change based on the state of an animation.

- **Each step of the animation:** You generally won't care about each step because there would simply be too much noise. However, if building a game, it might be useful to know whether an element is close to or intersecting another element on the page. (Yes, you can build Pong by using JavaScript.)

- **The end of the animation:** This is the moment you'll want to tie into to remove elements on the page, add new elements, or perform an Ajax call.

Looking at the API, you need to add the new code to the `animate()` function because it knows when the animation is at the beginning, when it's at the end, and when it makes each step in the animation. Why not add the start and end callbacks in the `start()` and `stop()` methods? Because the object can be stopped and restarted mid-animation, and adding it in those places doesn't properly account for that capability. You could add callbacks for all methods of the API, but that's not as necessary. You can always execute your own function any time you execute the API method. What you can't predict is when an animation is necessarily started, stopped, or stepped—thus the callbacks.

Let's add in the additional code, for which only the `animate()` function is shown (because it's the only function that needs to be modfied):

```
function animate()
{
    // what the new position will be
    var newval = options.from - (step * interval);
    // the step increments AFTER the comparison
    // check if the property exists and if the step
    // is 0 (the first step)
    if(options.onStart && step == 0) options.onStart();
    if(options.onStep) options.onStep();
    if(step++ <= numsteps) {
        // use Math.ceil to round to an integer and style
        el.style[options.property] =  Math.ceil(newval) + 'px';
    }else{
        el.style[options.property] =  options.to + 'px';
        if(options.onEnd) options.onEnd();
        publicMethods.stop();
    }
}
```

The `options` object now has some additional properties that you can pass in:

```
var options = {
    element:document.getElementById('elementID'),
    property:'height',
    from: 0,
    to: 200,
    duration: 1000,
    onStart: function(){ console.log('started') },
    onStep: function(){ console.log('stepped') },
    onEnd: function(){ console.log('ended') }
};
```

Keep in mind that `console.log()` was used within these functions only to track when the calls get made. As covered in Chapter 1, `console.log()` is a debugging technique that's not available in all browsers including Internet Explorer (IE) or Opera.

Queuing Animations

Queuing animations enables you to set up a sequence of events. To do this, you can actually take advantage of the callbacks made available to you within the animation object to script a number of animations to occur.

Let's say you have three elements side by side that you want to reveal one at a time. To do so, simply set the `onEnd` callback on the first object to start the animation on the second object, and set the `onEnd` callback on the second object to start the animation on the third object. Just like that, they'll cascade through until the end:

```
  var options1 = {
      element:document.getElementById('element1'),
      property:'height',
      from: 0,
      to: 200,
      duration: 1000,
      onEnd: function(){ a2.start(); }
   };
 var a1 = new Animation( options1 );

 var options2 = {
      element: document.getElementById('element2'),
      property:'height',
      from: 0,
      to: 200,
      duration: 1000,
      onEnd: function(){ a3.start(); }
   };
 var a2 = new Animation( options2 );

 var options3 = {
      element: document.getElementById('element3'),
      property:'height',
      from: 0,
      to: 200,
      duration: 1000
   };
 var a3 = new Animation( options3 );

 // start everything
 a1.start();
```

This code creates a sequence that looks similar to Figure 6-3.

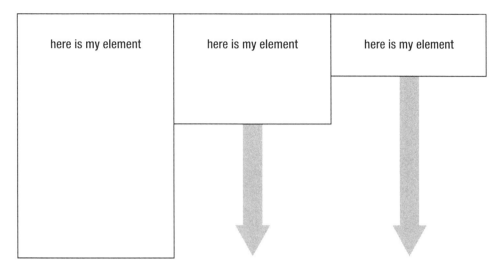

Figure 6-3. *Animating elements*

Extending the Animation Class

With the basic animation object in place, you can create a class that tackles a specific need. Suppose you have a set of frequently asked questions (FAQ) on your page that continue down the page like this: question—answer—question—answer.

The animation object on its own doesn't quite have everything you need. First and foremost, you need to be able to remember the height of the object so that you know how big to make it again after you've hidden the answer. Also, because the object has only two states—open or closed—you'll keep track of the state you're in and toggle between them.

Call the new class Toggler, which will take just one argument: the element that will control the toggle:

```
function Toggler(element){ }
```

Take a quick look at what the HTML for this FAQ would look like. Each question has a class name of question. In this example, each answer has a class name of answer, but it's not really necessary (as you'll see in a moment):

```
<div class="question">Question 1</div>
<div class="answer">Lengthy description ... </div>
<div class="question">Question 2</div>
<div class="answer">Lengthy description ... </div>
<div class="question">Question 3</div>
<div class="answer">Lengthy description ... </div>
<div class="question">Question 4</div>
<div class="answer">Lengthy description ... </div>
```

When the window loads, you need to get all the question elements and create new Toggler options with each one. This code uses the getElementsByClassName() function that was covered in Chapter 2:

```
var els = getElementsByClassName(document, 'question');
for(var i=0;i<els.length;i++)
{
  new Toggler(els[i]);
}
```

Now that you've created a bunch of new `Toggler` objects, you need to add some meat to the `Toggler` class—you have to find the answer for the question selected. In this case, the answer always appears right after the question. To retrieve the answer, simply use the DOM property `nextSibling`. As you might remember, IE doesn't count the empty text node between the two nodes. Therefore, to ensure that all browsers get to the answer, check to see whether you have an element; if not, grab the next element. You'll also grab the initial height of the answer and store it for later.

```
function Toggler(element){
  var answer = element.nextSibling;
  if(answer.nodeType !=1) answer = answer.nextSibling;
  var startHeight = answer.offsetHeight;
  var hidden = false;
}
```

Next, add the code that actually does the toggling. The toggle will instantiate a new animation object each time by swapping the `to` and `from` options to control the direction:

```
function Toggler(element){
  var answer = element.nextSibling;
  if(answer.nodeType !=1) answer = answer.nextSibling;
  var startHeight = answer.offsetHeight;
  var hidden = false;

  function toggle()
  {
    var start, stop;
    if(hidden)
    {
      start = 0;
      stop = startHeight;
    }else{
      start = startHeight;
      stop = 0;
    }

    var options = {
      element: answer,
      from:start,
      to:stop,
      duration:250,
      property:'height'
    };
```

```
    // instantiate and start the animation
    (new Animation(options)).start()
    // toggle the hidden property
    hidden = hidden ? false : true;
  }
}
```

With the `toggle` function defined, you need to add the last two ingredients (attaching the event handler and hiding the answer to start off with):

```
function Toggler(element){
  var answer = element.nextSibling;
  if(answer.nodeType !=1) answer = answer.nextSibling;
  var startHeight = answer.offsetHeight;
  var hidden = false;

  function toggle()
  {
    var start, stop;
    if(hidden)
    {
      start = 0;
      stop = startHeight;
    }else{
      start = startHeight;
      stop = 0;
    }

    var options = {
      element: answer,
      from:start,
      to:stop,
      duration:250,
      property:'height'
    };
    // instantiate and start the animation
    (new Animation(options)).start()
    // toggle the hidden property
    hidden = hidden ? false : true;
  }

  element.onclick = toggle;
  toggle();
}
```

Add a little bit of CSS:

```
.question {
  font-weight:bold;
  margin-top:10px;
  cursor:pointer; /* use the same pointer as a link */
}

.answer {
  /* must be overflow hidden to do the animation */
  overflow:hidden;
}
```

And just like that, you've got a handy way to handle the FAQ, as demonstrated in Figure 6-4.

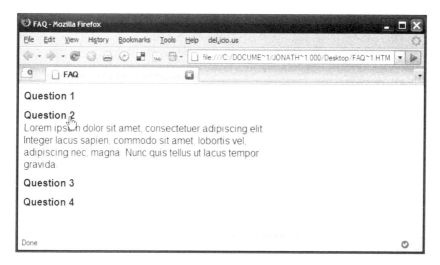

Figure 6-4. *The FAQ with one item expanded*

Note You'll see more FAQ magic in Chapter 8, which contains an FAQ case study.

Using Libraries for Animation

Even though you've put together a pretty decent little class of your own, there are still a number of areas to tackle, which is why libraries are beneficial: they have already solved a lot of the problems.

Take for example, modifying the opacity of an object. Unlike other properties, such as left or top, opacity takes a value only between 0 and 1 and isn't a pixel-based measurement. Therefore, you have to start adding in special cases, checking for property values being passed in and planning for them.

You'll now take a look at a few of the different animation options available to use through the following libraries:

- Script.aculo.us

- jQuery

- Mootools

Script.aculo.us

The Script.aculo.us library extends Prototype to offer up a number of animation possibilities through its core and combination effect components.

Similar to the animation object you developed previously, there is a base effect class, called `Effect.Base`, from which all the other effect classes extend. It's slightly different in that the base class doesn't actually change the value of any object, but is instead left up to the child classes. The base class handles all the timing, which enables each child class to do what it does best and account for the special scenarios (such as the opacity issue).

The core effects are as follows:

- `Effect.Opacity`: Changes the opacity of an element, enabling it to fade in or out

- `Effect.Move`: Moves an element around the page

- `Effect.Scale`: Scales the element up by resizing its dimensions and the font size of the content within

- `Effect.Highlight`: Adjusts the background color, usually from a bright color to the default color (highlights status changes)

- `Effect.ScrollTo`: Scrolls the window to a particular location on the page (useful for those anchored links mentioned earlier)

The combination effects that build on top of the core events are the following:

- `Effect.Fade`

- `Effect.Appear`

- `Effect.Puff`

- `Effect.BlindUp`

- `Effect.BlindDown`

- `Effect.SwitchOff`

- `Effect.DropOut`

- `Effect.Shake`

- `Effect.SlideDown`

- `Effect.SlideUp`

- `Effect.Squish`

- Effect.Grow

- Effect.Shrink

- Effect.Pulsate

- Effect.Fold

- Effect.Morph

Effects are instantiated by passing the element or the element ID into the constructor:

`new Effect.Puff('elementID');`

Each class takes an `options` object as the second parameter, but the options will vary from class to class.

The Script.aculo.us web site includes a demo of each of these effects (`http://wiki. script.aculo.us/scriptaculous/show/CombinationEffectsDemo`) if you want to see them in action (see Figure 6-5).

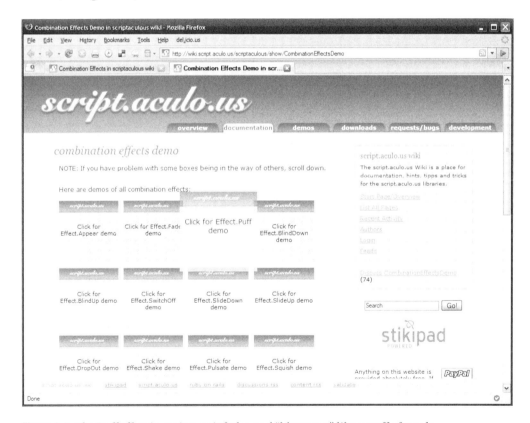

Figure 6-5. *The Puff effect in action as it fades and "blows out" like a puff of smoke*

If you're already using Prototype on a project that includes Prototype and Script.aculo.us by default (for example, a Ruby on Rails project), adding Script.aculo.us effects is super simple.

jQuery

This extremely compact library (only 20K) can do a number of straightforward animations out of the box. jQuery is great for adding simple animations because of its structure. Just pull out one or more elements and then use any of the animation objects to animate.

The standard jQuery animations include the following:

- `fadeIn()`, `fadeOut()`, and `fadeTo()`: These animations enable you to fade an object in and out or fade from the current value to a predefined value.

- `slideDown()`, `slideUp()`, and `slideToggle()`: These animations have the same effects as the FAQ example you did earlier, expanding and collapsing a section of the page. `slideToggle()` toggles an element between `slideDown()` and `slideUp()`.

- `show()`, `hide()`, and `toggle()`: `show()` and `hide()` fade and resize the element; `toggle()` switches between showing and hiding the item.

These effects are really easy to use and can be tweaked by specifying the speed of the animation as `'slow'`, `'normal'`, `'fast'`, or the number of milliseconds for the animation. You can add a second parameter, which is the callback function to be called upon completion of the animation.

```
$('#elementID').fadeOut('fast', function(){
  alert("I'm done the animation")
});
```

jQuery also offers up an `animate()` method that enables you to change multiple properties at the same time. The properties to change are contained in an object literal and passed as the first parameter. The second parameter is speed, the next is the easing effect, and the last is the callback function. Only the first parameter is required; the others are optional. jQuery even tries (and succeeds) to be smart and enables any of the optional parameters to appear in any order.

```
$("#elementID").animate(
  { height: 'toggle', opacity: 'toggle' },
  "fast",
  "easein",
  function(){alert('done!');}
);
```

Note Easing uses mathematics to adjust the speed of the animation over time. The animation might start slowly and then speed up as it gets close to the end (or vice versa), creating a more natural feel than an animation that doesn't change in speed.

Easing effects are handled via a jQuery plug-in, which is an additional function that ties into the jQuery namespace. The supported easing effects are handled by the jQuery Easing Plugin, available from `http://gsgd.co.uk/sandbox/jquery.easing.php`. Common easing effects include `easein` and `easeout`, along with fancier effects such as `bouncein/bounceout` and `backin/backout`.

You can find more jQuery plug-ins at `http://docs.jquery.com/Plugins`.

Mootools

Mootools is made by the same folks who gave you Moo.fx, which gained popularity because it was small (3K), came with a compact version of Prototype dubbed Prototype Lite (5K), and focused strictly on animations. This time around, the developers dropped the Prototype requirement and created a variety of useful components. The effects are broken down into a number of components (similar to Script.aculo.us).

The `Fx.Base` is very similar to Script.aculo.us, with the other classes extending it as need be. Of the `Fx` classes, only three offer up specific animation functionality:

- `Fx.Style`: Modifies an element style property over time

- `Fx.Scroll`: Scrolls the window or an element with `overflow:scroll`

- `Fx.Slide`: Shows or hides content using a slide animation

The other `Fx` classes are utility classes to handle various animation duties such as transitions (`Fx.Transitions`) or applying multiple style effects to multiple elements at once (`Fx.Elements`). The `Style` object resembles your approach in that the animation begins only after the `start()` method is executed.

```
var anim = new Fx.Style('elementID', left',{duration:500});
anim.start(0, 100);
```

Summary

There can be a place for visual effects in your work because they can solve usability issues inherent within even standard web pages. You built your own animation class and in the process discovered many of the concepts discussed over the last few chapters. Finally, you saw how the popular JavaScript libraries handle animation and which additional features they have to offer up.

In Chapter 7, Stuart Langridge takes a good look at one of the most common uses for DOM scripting: form validation.

CHAPTER 7

■ ■ ■

Form Validation and JavaScript

By Stuart Langridge

Most web applications use the `<form>` tag at one place or another. If your app uses a `<form>` to gather information, you'll probably want to try and validate that information to make sure that what the user is filling in is reasonable in some way. Hence the convention that an * next to a bit of a form means "this part is mandatory; you must fill it in." It's equally important that if you want the information you receive to be in a certain format you have your app enforce that format. This is what validation is all about: having your app check what the user types to confirm that it's what you were expecting. If you're asking users for the number of chickens they own, it's a good idea to check that what they type in is a number instead of "I don't own any chickens," or something similar.

Validation helps with data quality. It also means that later bits of your programs can assume that the data they have is valid; for example, if you want to sell the user another chicken, you can write "How would you like to own ($chickens + 1) chickens?" without having to worry about what happens if you try to add 1 to what the user typed in. Validation is important.

Since this is a book about document object model (DOM) scripting, you might think that you'll launch immediately into JavaScript, but that's not the case. One of the important points about validation on the Web is that you must not just use JavaScript to do it. Users might have JavaScript turned off; they might be using their cell phone; they might be demonstrating your magnificent chickenbuyer.example.com site to someone on a train using a Blackberry. Validation must take place on the server as well as on the client. So first you'll briefly look at server-based validation, and then at how and why to extend it to JavaScript.

Doing It on the Server

You'll use regular expressions here to check a form submission. The examples in Listing 7-1 are PHP, but every language now includes support for regular expressions; simply adapt for your choice of server-side technology. If you're not familiar with regular expressions, there are guides galore on the Web: `http://www.regular-expressions.info/` is a good introduction that goes into a decent level of detail. The canonical written reference is Jeffrey Friedl's *Mastering Regular Expressions*, described at `http://regex.info/`.

Listing 7-1. simple-form.php *shows validation of a simple form in PHP*

```php
<?php

$VALIDATIONS = Array(
  "firstname" => Array("regexp" => '.+', "error" => "Enter a name"),
  "lastname" => Array("regexp" => '.+', "error" => "Enter a name"),
  "heads" => Array("regexp" => '^\d+$', "error" => "Number of heads ➥
 should be a whole number"),
  "dob" => Array("regexp" => '^\d\d[\/.-]\d\d[\/.-]\d\d\d\d$', "error" => ➥
"Enter dates in  format DD/MM/YYYY"),
  "email" => Array("regexp" => '^.+@.+\..+$', "error" => ➥
"This address is not valid")
);

$ERRORS = Array();

if (isset($_GET["submit"])) {
  # form was submitted
  foreach ($VALIDATIONS as $field => $data) {
    if (!isset($_GET[$field])) continue; # skip any that aren't sent

    $regexpstr = $data["regexp"];

    if (preg_match("/$regexpstr/", $_GET[$field]) == 0) {
      $ERRORS[$field] = $data["error"];
    }
  }

  if (count($ERRORS) == 0) echo "Data OK; now redirect!";
}
?>


<!DOCTYPE HTML PUBLIC "-//W3C//DTD HTML 4.01//EN"
"http://www.w3.org/TR/html4/strict.dtd">
<html>
<head>

<title>A simple PHP form using regular expressions for validation</title>
<link rel="stylesheet" href="styles.css">
</head>

<body>
<h1>A simple PHP form using regular expressions for validation</h1>
<form>
 <p><label for="firstname">First name</label>
    <input type="text" id="firstname" name="firstname">
    <span class="error">
```

```
      <?php if (array_key_exists("firstname",$ERRORS)) echo $ERRORS["firstname"]; ?>
    </span>
</p>

<p><label for="lastname">Last name</label>
    <input type="text" id="lastname" name="lastname">
    <span class="error">
      <?php if (array_key_exists("lastname",$ERRORS)) echo $ERRORS["lastname"]; ?>
    </span>
</p>

<p><label for="heads">Number of heads</label>
    <input type="text" id="heads" name="heads">
    <span class="error">
      <?php if (array_key_exists("heads",$ERRORS)) echo $ERRORS["heads"]; ?>
    </span>
</p>

<p><label for="dob">Date of birth (DD/MM/YYYY)</label>
    <input type="text" id="dob" name="dob">
    <span class="error">
      <?php if (array_key_exists("dob",$ERRORS)) echo $ERRORS["dob"]; ?>
    </span>
</p>

<p><label for="email">Email address of someone you don't like for
    spamming purposes</label>
    <input type="text" id="email" name="email">
    <span class="error">
      <?php if (array_key_exists("email",$ERRORS)) echo $ERRORS["email"]; ?>
    </span>
</p>

<p><input type="submit" name="submit" value="Send answers"></p>
</form>
</body>
</html>
```

The `simple-form.php` file is a very basic example of how you might do regexp-based validation in PHP on the server. Each field is given a regexp to match against what the user submits and an error message to display if it doesn't match. For example, the "number of heads" field must contain digits, so its regexp is ^\d+$. (Note the +, meaning "one or more of these," which makes this field compulsory.) If completing the field were optional (so it could be left blank), the regexp would have been ^\d*$ because * means "zero or more of these."

Note also that some of these regexps are fairly simplistic. Regular expressions are good but imperfect tools. For example, the e-mail regexp—^.+@.+\..+$—allows invalid nastinesses such as `stuart@somewhere@somewhere@somewhere.com`. You often cannot completely rely on a regexp to give you validity. `http://www.ex-parrot.com/~pdw/Mail-RFC822-Address.html` has a "proper" regexp for matching e-mail addresses, which is a mighty 6251 characters long. In practice, what you're doing with validation here is stripping out things that are obviously wrong, not trying to catch every single invalid case.

The Client Side

On to JavaScript. JavaScript supports regexps natively; a string has a `search()` method that takes a regexp as parameter and returns the first character where the regexp is found in the string, or `-1` if it's not found at all. That being the case, then, you need JavaScript to do the following:

1. Define the list of regular expressions and the fields to which they apply.

2. On page load, attach an `onBlur` handler to each field that has an applicable regexp.

3. The `onBlur` handler, which runs when the user's focus leaves a field, should check what the user has entered in that field against the regexp.

4. If the regexp doesn't match what users enter, display an error message so they know they've entered something incorrectly.

Note that you're hooking up the JavaScript validation to the fields on page load, following the DOM scripting principles of unobtrusiveness and progressive enhancement. If the user doesn't have JavaScript, the hookup won't happen, but because you're already validating on the server, the validation still happens and the page isn't broken. Equally, you're not mixing lots of JavaScript code in with the HTML markup; the script is self-contained in a `<script>` tag in the page header.

Since you already have the list of fields and regular expressions in PHP, it would be good to have the PHP dynamically write out that list in a form that JavaScript can understand (so it doesn't have to be entered twice). JavaScript natively supports regexps; you can define a regexp in JavaScript by putting slashes around it (for example, `/^hello$/`). So the structure you want to create in JavaScript should look something like this:

```
VALIDATIONS = {
  "firstname": { 'regexp': /.+/, 'error': 'Enter a name' },
  "lastname": { 'regexp': /.+/, 'error': 'Enter a name' },
  "heads": { 'regexp': /^\d+$/,
    'error': 'Number of heads should be a whole number' }
};
```

This can be written out directly into the `<script>` tag by the server-side PHP, so you don't need to define the list twice. The code in Listing 7-2 does exactly this; the PHP iterates through the PHP `$VALIDATIONS` array and writes out the equivalent JavaScript associative array.

The next step is to walk through the list of validations, find each associated field, and attach an `onBlur` handler:

```
for (fieldname in VALIDATIONS) {
  fld = document.getElementById(fieldname);
  if (!fld) continue; // ignore this field if it doesn't exist in the page
  addEvent(fld, "blur", checkField);
}
```

VALIDATIONS is an associative array (sometimes called a hash table or a dictionary), which means that you can walk through its keys with for (key in VALIDATIONS), a useful technique. The keys of the array are the field names, which is what you care about, so for each one you fetch the page element with that ID (exiting if there is no element with that ID), and then set the function checkField() to be the event handler for the blur event.

The checkField() function implements steps 3 and 4 in the requirements list—checking what the user entered in a field against the field's regexp, and displaying an error message if it doesn't match. It looks like this:

```
function checkField(e) {

  fld = window.event ? window.event.srcElement : e.target;

  fieldname = fld.id;

  if (VALIDATIONS[fieldname]) {
    re = VALIDATIONS[fieldname]["regexp"];

    if (fld.value.search(re) == -1) {
      // the regular expression didn't match
      // find the span.error element for this field
      // and put the error message in it

      span = fld.parentNode.getElementsByTagName('span')[0];
      span.innerHTML = VALIDATIONS[fieldname]["error"];
    } else {
      // the regular expression *did* match
      // remove the error message!

      span = fld.parentNode.getElementsByTagName('span')[0];
      span.innerHTML = "";
    }
  }
}
```

First, since this is an event handler, you need to get the element that fired the event—in this case, that element will be the text field itself, which is what you care about. You use a little cross-browser coding to get a reference to the element, using the window.event object in browsers that provide it (Internet Explorer) and the World Wide Web Consortium (W3C) event object in other browsers.

Following that, you look in the VALIDATIONS object to see whether there's a regexp defined for this field by checking whether VALIDATIONS[fieldname] exists. If it does, you retrieve the regexp defined in VALIDATIONS, ready for checking.

Text fields have their current value available in fieldobject.value, which is a string, and strings (as noted previously) have a search() method to check the string against a regexp that returns -1 if there's no match. So the following means "if the value in this field does not match the regexp," and that's when the error message needs to be displayed:

```
if (fld.value.search(re) == -1)
```

The page has been built so that the part containing this field looks like the following:

```
<p><label for="dob">Date of birth (DD/MM/YYYY)</label>

    <input type="text" id="dob" name="dob">
    <span class="error"></span>
</p>
```

So each field has an associated span for displaying the error messages. The DOM tree for that snippet, then, would be that the <label>, the <input>, and the <span> are all children of the <p> element. So the best way to get a reference to the <span> is with the following:

```
fld.parentNode.getElementsByTagName('span')[0]
```

At that point, you can simply set the appropriate error message to display by setting the innerHTML of the <span>. Similarly, when the if statement that checks the field against the regexp returns something other than -1, it means that the field value is correct, so you can remove the error message by setting the innerHTML of <span> to blank.

Finally, you add a cross-browser addEvent() function and wrap the whole block of JavaScript code up in a simple object (so that the function names and variables don't collide with any other scripts you happen to be loading), and tidy up the PHP a tiny bit (printing a field with a function instead of having all the fields directly inline in the page), and you have Listing 7-2.

Listing 7-2. simple-form-tidier-js.php *adds JavaScript regular expression validation to* simple-form.php

```
<?php
$VALIDATIONS = Array(
  "firstname" => Array("regexp" => '.+', "error" => "Enter a name"),
  "lastname" => Array("regexp" => '.+', "error" => "Enter a name"),
  "heads" => Array("regexp" => '^\d+$',
                  "error" => "Number of heads should be a whole number"),
    "dob" => Array("regexp" => '^\d\d[\/.-]\d\d[\/.-]\d\d\d\d$',
                  "error" => "Enter dates in  format DD/MM/YYYY"),
  "email" => Array("regexp" => '^.+@.+\..+$',
                  "error" => "This address is not valid")
);
```

```php
$ERRORS = Array();

if (isset($_GET["submit"])) {
  # form was submitted

  foreach ($VALIDATIONS as $field => $data) {
    if (!isset($_GET[$field])) continue; # skip any that aren't sent

    $regexpstr = $data["regexp"];

    if (preg_match("/$regexpstr/", $_GET[$field]) == 0) {
      $ERRORS[$field] = $data["error"];
    }

  }

  if (count($ERRORS) == 0) echo "Data OK; now redirect!";
}

?>
```

```html
<!DOCTYPE HTML PUBLIC "-//W3C//DTD HTML 4.01//EN"
"http://www.w3.org/TR/html4/strict.dtd">

<html>
<head>

<title>A simple PHP form using regular expressions for validation</title>

<link rel="stylesheet" href="styles.css">

<script type="text/javascript">
validator = {

  VALIDATIONS: {
```

```php
<?php

    foreach ($VALIDATIONS as $field => $data) {

      $regexpstr = $data["regexp"];

      $errorstr = $data["error"];
      echo "\"$field\": { 'regexp': /$regexpstr/, 'error': '$errorstr' },\n";
```

```
      }
  ?>
    },

  init: function() {
    // check this browser has the chops to do the DOM scripting we need

    if (!document.getElementById) return;

    // Walk through the VALIDATIONS list and for each one find the field
    //  it applies to and attach an onBlur handler, so when the user leaves
    //  the field, it checks the contents of the field against the regexp.

    for (fieldname in validator.VALIDATIONS) {
      fld = document.getElementById(fieldname);

      if (!fld) continue; // ignore this field if it doesn't exist in the page

      validator.addEvent(fld, "blur", validator.checkField);
    }
  },

  checkField: function(e) {
    fld = window.event ? window.event.srcElement : e.target;

    fieldname = fld.id;

    if (validator.VALIDATIONS[fieldname]) {
      re = validator.VALIDATIONS[fieldname]["regexp"];

      if (fld.value.search(re) == -1) {
        // the regular expression didn't match
        // find the span.error element for this field
        // and put the error message in it

        span = fld.parentNode.getElementsByTagName('span')[0];
        span.innerHTML = validator.VALIDATIONS[fieldname]["error"];
      } else {
        // the regular expression *did* match
        // remove the error message!

        span = fld.parentNode.getElementsByTagName('span')[0];
        span.innerHTML = "";
      }
    }
  },
```

```
    addEvent: function( obj, type, fn ) {
      if (obj.addEventListener) {
        obj.addEventListener( type, fn, false );
      } else if (obj.attachEvent) {
        obj["e"+type+fn] = fn;
        obj[type+fn] = function() { obj["e"+type+fn]( window.event ); }
        obj.attachEvent( "on"+type, obj[type+fn] );
      }
    }
}

validator.addEvent(window, "load", validator.init);

</script>
</head>

<body>

<h1>A simple PHP form using regular expressions for validation</h1>

<form>

<?php
function field($name, $text) {

  global $ERRORS;

  echo "<p><label for=\"$name\"";

  if (array_key_exists($name,$ERRORS)) {
    echo " class=\"error\"";
  }

  echo ">$text</label>\n";
  echo "<input type=\"text\" id=\"$name\" name=\"$name\">\n";

  if (array_key_exists($name,$ERRORS)) {
    $err = $ERRORS[$name];

    echo "<span class=\"error\">$err</span>";
    } else {
    echo "<span class=\"error\"></span>";
    }

  echo "</p>\n";
}
```

```
field("firstname", "First name");
field("lastname", "Last name");
field("heads", "Number of heads");
field("dob", "Date of birth (DD/MM/YYYY)");
field("email", "Email address of someone you don't like for spamming purposes");
?>


  <p><input type="submit" name="submit" value="Send answers"></p>

</form>
</body>
</html>
```

And there you have it: form validation with regular expressions, progressively enhanced to use DOM scripting.

Now that there's an infrastructure in place to do the validation of this form, there are numerous ways to add extra enhancements. Here I'll discuss two: having the page add the error span itself (instead of requiring it to already be present in the HTML) and preventing the form being submitted if there are errors.

Adding the Error Span from JavaScript

In Listing 7-2, the PHP server code writes out a `<span class="error"></span>` for each field, even when there aren't any errors, as a placeholder for the error message. While these spans are empty and hence don't contribute to page layout, it's a little inelegant, and they clutter the resultant HTML. It would be tidier if the JavaScript added and removed the spans itself. Remember that you can't just assume that JavaScript detecting an error means that you should add a span—if the server code detects an error it will correctly write out that error message. So, on detecting an error, the script needs to check whether there's an error span already present. If there is, alter its content; if there isn't, create one.

Listing 7-3 is a relatively simple addition to the existing Listing 7-2; nothing needs to change other than the JavaScript `checkField()` function.

Listing 7-3. `checkField()` *from* `simple-form-tidier-js-create-spans.php`

```
checkField: function(e) {
  fld = window.event ? window.event.srcElement : e.target;
  fieldname = fld.id;
  if (validator.VALIDATIONS[fieldname]) {
    re = validator.VALIDATIONS[fieldname]["regexp"];

    if (fld.value.search(re) == -1) {
      // the regular expression didn't match
      // find the span.error element for this field
      // and put the error message in it
      spans = fld.parentNode.getElementsByTagName('span');
```

```
    if (spans.length == 0) {
      // there is no error span, so, create one
      span = document.createElement('span');
      span.className = 'error';
      fld.parentNode.appendChild(span);
    } else {
      span = fld.parentNode.getElementsByTagName('span')[0];
    }
    span.innerHTML = validator.VALIDATIONS[fieldname]["error"];
  } else {
    // the regular expression *did* match
    // is there a span.error already?
    spans = fld.parentNode.getElementsByTagName('span');
    if (spans.length == 0) {
      // there is no error span, so do nothing
    } else {
      // remove the error span
      span = fld.parentNode.getElementsByTagName('span')[0];
      span.parentNode.removeChild(span);
      // and remove class="error" on the field's label, if it has it
      lbl = fld.parentNode.getElementsByTagName('label')[0];
      if (lbl.className == 'error') {
        lbl.className = lbl.className.replace(/\berror\b/,'');
      }
    }
  }
 }
}
```

The bold sections are those that have changed. The code to display an error message simply, instead of assuming that a span exists, checks to see whether it does exist (by looking for spans that are siblings of the text field). If it does not, the code creates the span with createElement() and inserts it into the document. Similarly, the code to remove the error message checks whether a span exists; if it does, the span is removed.

As a small extra wrinkle, the remove code also removes class="error" from the label if the server code put it there.

Preventing the Form Being Submitted

Another usability enhancement is to prevent the form from being submitted if there are errors present. It's generally good practice to stop the user from doing something if you *know* it's not going to work. If there's an error showing on the form you do indeed know that. However, it's something to be careful about; you don't want the form to remain unsubmittable if something goes wrong with the JavaScript checking or if JavaScript isn't available. First, then, you need a function that can enable or disable the submit button of the form—if there are errors showing, disable the button; if there are no errors, enable it. This is quite a simple function that doesn't depend on the current state of the button; if the button is already enabled, the function enables it again with no ill effects.

```
checkForErrors: function() {
  // Look for span.error in the page
  var spans = document.getElementsByTagName('span');
  for (var i=0; i<spans.length; i++) {
    // does this span have class=error?
    if (spans[i].className.match(/\berror\b/)) {
      // disable the submit button and exit
      document.getElementById("submitButton").disabled = true;
      return;
    }
  }
  // there were no span.error elements, so enable the submit button
  document.getElementById("submitButton").disabled = false;
}
```

To make the function's job easier, I also added an ID to the form's submit button.

The checkForErrors() function then needs to be called from a couple of different places. Whenever a field is checked (in the checkField() function), call checkForErrors(). It would be possible to be clever about this—call checkForErrors() only if the field's error status has changed from OK to error or the other way around—but it's often easier to understand if it's just called unconditionally, as you do here.

The function is also called when the JavaScript starts up from the init() function. This means that if the PHP code shows an error with the field, the submit button will be immediately disabled until the error is fixed. Importantly, the button is disabled *by JavaScript*; if the button is disabled by the PHP, and JavaScript isn't turned on, there is no way to re-enable it. It's important that you maintain this separation between server-side code and client-side code; don't do things on the server that require client-side code to put right or to alter because they won't work in scriptless environments.

Listing 7-4 shows this code in practice, with the (minimal) changes in bold.

Listing 7-4. simple-form-tidier-js-prevent-submission.php

```
...
<html>
<head>
<title>A simple PHP form using regular expressions for validation</title>
<link rel="stylesheet" href="styles.css">
<script type="text/javascript">

...

  init: function() {
    // check this browser has the chops to do the DOM scripting we need
    if (!document.getElementById) return;
```

```
    // Walk through the VALIDATIONS list and for each one find the field
    //  it applies to and attach an onBlur handler, so when the user leaves
    //  the field, it checks the contents of the field against the regexp.
    for (fieldname in validator.VALIDATIONS) {
      fld = document.getElementById(fieldname);
      if (!fld) continue; // ignore this field if it doesn't exist in the page
      validator.addEvent(fld, "blur", validator.checkField);
    }
    validator.checkForErrors();
  },

  checkField: function(e) {
    ...
    // finally, disable or enable the submit button as appropriate
    validator.checkForErrors();
  },

  checkForErrors: function() {
    // Look for span.error in the page
    var spans = document.getElementsByTagName('span');
    for (var i=0; i<spans.length; i++) {
      // does this span have class=error?
      if (spans[i].className.match(/\berror\b/)) {
        // disable the submit button and exit
        document.getElementById("submitButton").disabled = true;
        return;
      }
    }
    // there were no span.error elements, so enable the submit button
    document.getElementById("submitButton").disabled = false;
  },

  addEvent: function( obj, type, fn ) {
    ...
  }
}
</script>
</head>

<body>
<h1>A simple PHP form using regular expressions for validation</h1>
<form>

 ...
 <p><input type="submit" name="submit" id="submitButton" value="Send answers"></p>
</form>
</body>
</html>
```

Form Validation with Ajax

Regular expressions are a powerful tool, but they do have their limitations. In the previous example, the date expression was ^\d\d[\/.-]\d\d[\/.-]\d\d\d\d$, which allows two digits, a separator, two digits, a separator, and four digits. This will correctly block something similar to "I'm not telling you my date of birth", but it will merrily allow such invalid monstrosities as "99/99/9999", "32/01/1995", and "29/02/2007". Writing a regular expression to correctly trap all these cases would be impossible. There are also plenty of things that can't be checked with a regular expression at all: for example, freeform date fields, numbers with a range, or URLs (you can check that something looks like a URL, but not whether that URL actually works). For checking this sort of user entry, you need real code.

Doing It on the Server

It's pretty easy to put together a server-side form in which each field is tied to a particular function that validates what's entered into it. A little PHP example is shown in Listing 7-5.

Listing 7-5. noajax-form.php *demonstrates PHP server-side validation*

```php
<?php

require_once "validation.php";

$ERRORS = Array();

if (isset($_GET["submit"])) {

  # form was submitted

  foreach ($_GET as $field => $data) {
    $check = validate($field, $data);

    if ($check != "") {
      $ERRORS[$field] = $check;
    }
  }

  if (count($ERRORS) == 0) echo "Data OK; now redirect!";
}
?>

<!DOCTYPE HTML PUBLIC "-//W3C//DTD HTML 4.01//EN"
"http://www.w3.org/TR/html4/strict.dtd">

<html>
```

```
<head>
<title>A simple PHP form using separate code for validation</title>
<link rel="stylesheet" href="styles.css">
</head>

<body>
<h1>A simple PHP form using separate code for validation</h1>

<form>

 <p><label for="dayofyear">Favourite day of the year (1-365)</label>
    <input type="text" id="dayofyear" name="dayofyear">
    <span class="error">
    <?php if (array_key_exists("dayofyear",$ERRORS)) echo $ERRORS["dayofyear"]; ?>
    </span>
 </p>

 <p><label for="date">Favourite date of all time</label>
    <input type="text" id="date" name="date">
    <span class="error">
    <?php if (array_key_exists("date",$ERRORS)) echo $ERRORS["date"]; ?>
    </span>
 </p>

 <p><label for="word">Favourite word</label>
    <input type="text" id="word" name="word">
    <span class="error">
    <?php if (array_key_exists("word",$ERRORS)) echo $ERRORS["word"]; ?>
    </span>
 </p>

 <p><input type="submit" name="submit" value="Send answers"></p>
</form>

</body>
</html>
```

This code uses the $ERRORS approach and a form structure similar to the preceding regular expressions form, but it now calls a function validate() for each submitted form value. The validate() function is defined in a separate file (for reasons that will become clear in a moment), and it is more trivial PHP, as shown in Listing 7-6.

Listing 7-6. validation.php *contains the validation functions for each field*

```php
<?php

function validate($field, $value) {

  switch ($field) {

    case "dayofyear":
      if (is_numeric($value) && intval($value) > 0 && intval($value) <= 365) {
        return "";
      } else {
        return "Day of year must be between 1 and 365";
      }
      break;

    case "date":
      if (strtotime($value) === false) {
        return "Invalid date (try 10 September 2000, +1 week, or next Thursday)";
      } else {
        return "";
      }
      break;

    case "word":
      if ($value == "" || is_numeric($value)) {
        return "You must supply a favorite word";
      } else {
        return "";
      }
      break;

    default:
      return "";
  }
}
```

You pass a field name and a field value to the validate() function. It returns an empty string if the value is valid and an error message if it isn't. This function could obviously call other functions and be as complex as you like.

The Client Side

The advantage of having the validation routine separate from the page is that you can then enhance the form by having JavaScript check the validity of each field through an Ajax call to the server. In simple terms, it should work like this:

1. On page load, attach a handler to the `blur` event of each field.

2. The `onBlur` handler, which runs when the user's focus leaves a field, should grab the value out of the field and make an `XMLHttpRequest` call to the server, passing the field's name and field value.

3. The server then runs the validation code—this is exactly the same validation code that the form uses on the server side, not any kind of copy or duplicate of it—and returns the `validate()` function's result.

4. The JavaScript receives the result of the Ajax call, and if it's an error message, it updates the page with the error.

Again, it's important to note that there's only one `validate()` function. The server-side code calls it when doing validation of the form, and the enhanced form calls the same function via Ajax.

There are a number of parts to building this new form. The previous regular-expressions-based example didn't do anything hugely complicated in terms of JavaScript. With an Ajax-based approach you need to attach events, make an Ajax call, parse the results of the Ajax call into something meaningful, and update the DOM of the page. This is the ideal time to start thinking about introducing a JavaScript library to do some of the heavy lifting. All the libraries out there will make DOM manipulation and Ajax calls simple, and having a library do `XMLHttpRequest` is far easier than handling the complexities of it yourself in most cases.

For this example you'll use jQuery, which is very easy if the application you're building is on the Internet: simply add the following to the `<head>` of your page:

```
<script type="text/javascript"
        src="http://code.jquery.com/jquery-latest.pack.js"></script>
```

If you're building an internal application where your users won't have access to the Internet, you can download jQuery from `http://jquery.com`.

JSON is a convenient way to send small amounts of data back and forth to the server from JavaScript. You'll also use a library called Services_JSON (`http://mike.teczno.com/json.html`) that enables you to return JSON from the server in a convenient way so that you don't have to worry about the detail. Since you're sending only a field name and a value to the server, passing this information in the query string is the most convenient way. The server URL needs to extract this information from the query string, call the `validate()` function to validate it, and then return the results in the JSON format. In PHP, it would look something like Listing 7-7.

Listing 7-7. `ajax-validate.php` *calls the* `validate()` *function and returns the result as JSON*

```
<?php
require_once "validation.php";
require_once "JSON.php";

$field = $_GET["field"];
$value = $_GET["value"];
```

```php
if (!isset($field) || !isset($value)) {
  return_json("");
  die();
}

$check = validate($field, $value);

return_json($check);
die();

function return_json($data) {
  $json = new SERVICES_JSON();
  echo $json->encode($data);
}
?>
```

To test the Services_JSON PHP library visit the validate URL directly in your browser. Visiting `http://your_server_name/ajax-validate.php?field=dayofyear&value=invalid-value` will return the following:

```
"Day of year must be between 1 and 365", which is the correct error message.
```

There is built-in support in jQuery for requesting JSON data by Ajax with the `$.getJSON()` function. To request a URL and get back JSON data, use this call:

```javascript
$.getJSON("ajax-validate.php",{
  "field": "dayofyear",
  "value": "invalid-value"
}, function(data) {
  alert("this function is called with the JSON data: " + data);
});
```

As you can see, you pass the URL to fetch a JavaScript associative array of parameters that make up the query string and an inline callback function to call with the result.

Now you have everything you need to build the JavaScript half of the Ajax validation routine in your form. It's embarrassingly short:

```javascript
$(document).ready(function(){
  $('input[@type=text]').blur(function(){
    var thisfield = this;

    $.getJSON("ajax-validate.php",{
      "field": this.name,
      "value": this.value
    }, function(data) {
      $(thisfield).siblings("span.error").empty();
      if (!(data == "")) {
```

```
            $(thisfield).siblings("span.error").append(data);
        }
    });
  });
});
```

It may look complicated at first, but it's simply what you get when you combine the previous parts. A couple of extra wrinkles show up in this finished version, though.

The first is that inside a jQuery event handler, the element that the event actually *happened* on is called this. The code stores away a reference to this in a variable thisfield, so that it's still available in the callback.

A second wrinkle is that it's possible to create a jQuery query object from an existing variable by writing $(variable); this is used to make a query object from the stored thisfield variable.

The code makes use of another jQuery method: siblings(). This does the same thing as the fld.parentNode.getElementsByTagName('span')[0] part of the regular expression's code, but in a much easier-to-read way (I'm sure you'll agree). The siblings() method by itself will return all the other children of the same parent node, but you can pass a Cascading Style Sheets (CSS) selector as before to limit it to only the siblings you care about.

Finally, the empty() method is used to remove the contents of the error span, and the append() method fills in the error span with the error message passed back from the server if there was one.

Using Ajax to handle form validation is a convenient way to make your forms more usable; you avoid a page refresh and having to wait for the server to resend the whole page, but still take advantage of all the complexity and power of the code running on the server to make your validation routines as comprehensive as you want.

Summary

Form validation is important. If you care about the quality of your data, the best thing to do is to try and enforce that quality as much as possible. (And if you don't care, why collect it?) Although validation needs to happen on the server, it's good for users and for the feel and usability of your applications to have JavaScript-enhanced validation.

With a little extra work and help from a library or two, you can have your server-side validation also take place in the user's browser without having to duplicate all your validation functions in JavaScript.

May all your data gathering be valid from now on!

■■■

CHAPTER 8

Case Study: FAQ Facelift

By Aaron Gustafson

In the history of the Internet, there have been few things as constant as Frequently Asked Questions (FAQ) pages. Nearly every site has one, either in name or in spirit, and these pages really haven't changed much since they first appeared in the early 1990s.

Most FAQs take the form of a list of questions in which each is a link (using either an `id` or a `name` reference) to the applicable question/answer pair somewhere further down on the page, as seen in Figure 8-1. Maintenance of these FAQs can quickly become a nightmare because editors must not only create the question/answer pair but also then update the list at the top of the page (or on another page altogether). DRY principle be damned.

Note DRY: Don't Repeat Yourself.

Over the years, many of us have searched for a better way to manage FAQs, if only to make our lives a little easier. This case study will explore one way to give FAQs a facelift. With progressive enhancement in mind, you'll create a baseline, or low-fi, experience using just markup. Then you'll add a layer of interaction that relies solely on Cascading Style Sheets (CSS) for a hi-fi experience. Finally, you'll add a layer of interaction with JavaScript to kick it all into hi-def, or at least give it a little of that oh-so-popular Web 2.0 feel.

Note Jonathan introduced the concept of progressive enhancement in Chapter 7.

Your guinea pig will be the FAQ page for Firebug (`http://getfirebug.com`), the popular debugging extension for Firefox. You can find the files for this case study in `/starting files/`. The HTML file you'll be enhancing is `faq.html`, but you'll spend the majority of your time working in `faq.js` and `firebug.css`.

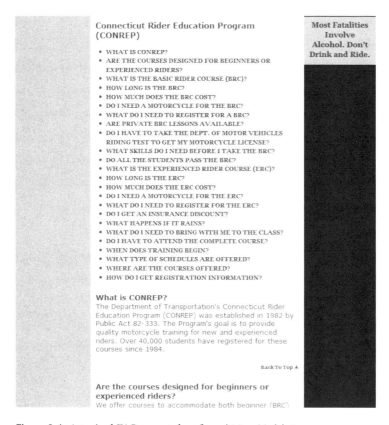

Figure 8-1. *A typical FAQ page taken from* `http://ride4ever.org`

Layer 1: Target Practice

A few years back, while experimenting with a definition list (dl) for marking up the question/answer pairs in an FAQ, it dawned on me that the extra list of questions at the top of FAQ pages wasn't needed. Using clever CSS, you can create the list effect by hiding the answers and showing them only when the appropriate question's link is clicked. It requires the use of a CSS3 pseudoclass selector (:target), but it is perfectly in keeping with the spirit of progressive enhancement.

Using a dl to mark up an FAQ looks something like this:

```
<dl>
  <dt><!-- QUESTION --></dt>
  <dd><!-- ANSWER --></dd>
  <dt><!-- QUESTION --></dt>
  <dd><!-- ANSWER --></dd>
  ...cut...
</dl>
```

And if you add a few hooks to the markup you can leverage :target to make the answers hidden by default, but visible when the corresponding link is clicked. The following is the way faq.html is constructed:

```
<dl class="faq">
  <dt><a href="#faq_1"><!-- QUESTION --></a></dt>
  <dd id="faq_1"><!-- ANSWER --></dd>
  <dt><a href="#faq_2"><!-- QUESTION --></a></dt>
  <dd id="faq_2"><!-- ANSWER --></dd>
  ...cut...
</dl>
```

I have already taken the lead and filled in this markup in faq.html. Open it up in a browser and take a look. You should see something akin to Figure 8-2.

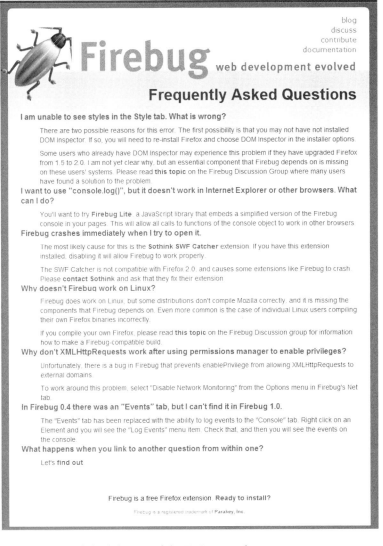

Figure 8-2. *The default layout of the FAQ example*

This is a perfectly usable document. Each question has an answer and, more importantly, each answer has an id that enables it to be bookmarked. Clicking any of the links will immediately jump the browser to that answer, which is just what you want.

Now open firebug.css and add the following styles at the bottom:

```css
.faq dt,
.faq dd {
  margin: 0;
  padding: 0;
}
.faq dd {
  margin-top: -3em;
  padding-top: 3.3em;
  position: absolute;
  top: 0;
  left: -999em;
}
.faq dd:target {
  position: static;
}
```

These rules did the following:

1. Reset the margin and padding on the definition term (dt) and definition data (dd) elements

2. Adjusted the margin-top on the dd to bring it up 3em (thereby overlapping the dt, so that the dt is still visible if the dd is linked to in the fragment identifier; that is, as a jump reference)

3. Adjusted the padding-top on the dd to push its contents down 3.3em so they are not overlapping the dt, to create a little breathing room

4. Positioned the dd absolutely (taking it out of the normal flow) and pushed it off the left side of the page so it is out of view (which is more accessible than display: none)

5. Set the dd to be statically positioned (that is, placed back in the normal flow) when it is the :target (the fragment identifier in the URI string)

Tip If you already use a universal reset in your style sheets, you can skip step 1.

Before you save the file and take a peek at the page again in a browser, add just a few more basic layout styles to keep the design from feeling too claustrophobic:

```
.faq dt {
  font-weight: bold;
  margin: 1em 0 0;
}
.faq dd > :last-child {
  margin-bottom: 0;
  padding-bottom: 0;
}
```

These styles will give the dt a little room on top and keep the last child of any of the dd elements from adding any unwanted gaps to the layout. Now save the file and refresh the browser to see your handiwork. You should see just the list of questions. Click a question, and the answer will be revealed, as shown in Figure 8-3. Internet Explorer (IE) 6 users will not see any change, but getting that problematic browser on track isn't too difficult and is covered in the sidebar.

Figure 8-3. *FAQ using* :target *shows the question you clicked in the open position.*

FIXING IE 6

Suckerfish Shoal (`http://tmldog.com/articles/suckerfish/shoal/`, by Patrick Griffiths and Dan Webb) and Dean Edwards' IE 7 scripts (`http://dean.edwards.name/IE7/`) will both enable IE 6 to apply target styles. If you have to overcome a lot of the IE 6 CSS and HTML shortcomings, the IE 7 scripts are my recommendation because they require no modifications to your style sheets to work.

It is recommended that you apply either fix by using conditional comments to avoid burdening more standards-compliant browsers with the extra download(s):

```
<!--[if IE lte 6]>
<script type="text/javascript" src="/js/ie7/ie7-core.js"></script>
<script type="text/javascript" src="/js/ie7/ie7-css3-selectors.js"></script>
<![endif]-->
```

This conditional comment serves `ie8-core.js` and `ie8-css3-selectors.js` to users of IE 6 and below.

Browsers that don't understand CSS get a nice listing of the questions and answers, with all the benefits of nice semantic markup, as seen in Figure 8-4.

Figure 8-4. *No CSS support, no problem.*

With the CSS-based interaction complete, you can move on to the really exciting bit: the JavaScript.

Layer 2: JavaScript Boogaloo

The CSS-based interaction you created is pretty good, but you can spruce it up and give it some flair. I've always liked the accordion-type effects that you see on some of the more Web 2.0-y sites, but that effect alone won't quite meet your needs. You can, however, use the basic concept and tailor it to your purposes. In this section, you'll create a JavaScript-based interaction for the FAQ that does the following:

- Triggers the answers to slide open when the corresponding question is clicked

- Enables one answer to reference another (triggering the reference to open without closing the original question, so the reference isn't lost)

- Keeps each question and answer pair bookmarkable

- Scrolls the window to bring focus to the newly opened answer

You'll use a few libraries and some other assorted helpers to get the job done:

- Prototype and Moo.fx for Prototype (`http://moofx.mad4milk.net/`) will provide some assistance to you in the general construction and animation of the script.

- To get the script going as soon as the page loads, you'll use Jesse Skinner's `addDOMLoadEvent()` (`www.thefutureoftheweb.com/blog/adddomloadevent`).

- To help you with debugging, I included jsTrace (`http://code.google.com/p/easy-designs/wiki/jsTrace`).

All this code has been included in the project files. Upon opening `faq.html`, you'll notice that the two libraries and jsTrace files (`dom-drag.js` and `jsTrace.js`) have already been included, as have `main.js` (containing the source for `addDOMLoadEvent()` and the `trace()` function for jsTrace, which you'll see in the next section) and `faq.js` (where you'll be building the FAQ object):

```
<script type="text/javascript" src="prototype.js"></script>
<script type="text/javascript" src="moo.fx.js"></script>
<script type="text/javascript" src="dom-drag.js"></script>
<script type="text/javascript" src="jsTrace.js"></script>
<script type="text/javascript" src="main.js"></script>
<script type="text/javascript" src="faq.js"></script>
```

Close that file and open up `faq.js`. Here you'll find the humble beginnings of the FAQ object:

```
var FAQ = {
  // open items
  open_items:     [],
  // running processes
  processes:      [],
  // timer wrapper
  timer:          new Object(),
  // what's opening
  to_open:        null,
```

```
// position we are scrolling to
scrolling_to:    null,
/* cache of where we are in the scrolling to keep us from
   trying to scroll again at the top or bottom */
scroll_cache:    null,

// ----- Initialization
initialize:      function(){
  // startup stuff
},

// ----- Open/Close/Complete
open:            function(){
  // opener
},
closeAndGo:      function(){
  // closer & scroll trigger
},
complete:        function( dd ){
  // housekeeping
},

// ----- Scrolling stuff
goTo:            function(){
  // scroll manager
},
/* Based on Travis Beckham's (squidfingers.com) smooth scroll
   with a little Shaun Inman (shauninman.com) thrown in */
getScrollLeft:   function(){
  if( document.all ){
    return ( document.documentElement.scrollLeft ) ?
             document.documentElement.scrollLeft :
             document.body.scrollLeft;
  } else {
    return window.pageXOffset;
  }
},
getScrollTop:    function(){
  if( document.all ){
    return ( document.documentElement.scrollTop ) ?
             document.documentElement.scrollTop :
             document.body.scrollTop;
  } else {
    return window.pageYOffset;
  }
},
scroll:          function(){
  // smooth scroll logic
},
```

```
// ----- Element Finder
getDT:            function(){
  // finds the DT associated with the DD
},

// ----- Process Management
processing:       function(){
  // let's us know if something is processing
},
wait:             function( method ){
  // makes a script wait to execute
}
};
```

You'll address each property and method of this object in turn, but I want to give you the general outline before you go too deep. As the comments mention, Travis Beckham (http:// squidfingers.com) and Shaun Inman (http://shauninman.com) provided a little code and a lot of inspiration for the scroll manager you'll build. With that shout-out complete, let's dive right in and start hacking away on FAQ.initialize().

Starting the Engine

The first thing the script needs to do is scan the document and grab any dl elements classified as faq so you can work your magic.

1. Using Prototype's $$() function, it's easy enough. Let's toss in a few trace() calls as well; it will give you a running tally of what's going on in the script. For more on using trace(), see the sidebar "Using jsTrace."

```
initialize:       function(){
  trace( 'initialize()' );
  // Collect the DLs & loop
  $$( 'dl.faq' ).each( function( dl ){
    trace( 'DL loop' );
    // magic goes here
  }.bind( this ) ); // End DL loop
},
```

■**Note** If you feel $$() is too slow for this purpose, you can always use old-school document object model (DOM) methods to do the same thing. Just be sure to make your results enumerable and then skip any dl that does not have a class of faq.

USING JSTRACE

Inspired by the `trace()` method in JavaScript's cousin, ActionScript, jsTrace is a web page overlay that provides a quick rundown on what's occurring in your scripts as it happens. To set it up, you simply define the `trace()` function and set it to send a message to the jsTrace window if jsTrace exists.

```
var trace;
if( typeof( jsTrace ) != 'undefined' ){
  trace = function( msg ){
    jsTrace.send( msg );
  };
} else {
  trace = function(){ };
}
```

By defining `trace()` as a null function when jsTrace is undefined, you make it safe to remove or comment out the jsTrace files without throwing JavaScript errors from `trace()` calls in the scripts. Of course, any `trace()` calls should be removed as part of your script-optimization regimen, but during the development process, it is very helpful to be able to turn jsTrace off and then on again easily.

You can also drag the jsTrace debugger window around to reposition it and grab the little triangle in the lower-right corner to resize it. You can also close it altogether by clicking the X in the upper-right corner. If you have cookies enabled, the size and position of the debugger will be maintained as well. So you can tuck it out of the way and won't have to move it each time you refresh.

2. Of course, you still haven't set up `FAQ.initialize()` to actually run yet, so you should do that as well. At the bottom of `faq.js`, add the following just after the closing brace of the object:

```
if( typeof( Prototype ) != 'undefined' &&
    typeof( fx ) != 'undefined' &&
    document.getElementsByTagName( 'dl' ) ){
  addDOMLoadEvent( function(){ FAQ.initialize(); } );
}
```

This sets `FAQ.initialize()` to run as soon as the DOM is loaded, but only if Prototype and Moo.fx are both defined and the document contains one or more dl elements. After all, the script will throw a lot of errors without the libraries, and there's no reason to run it if there are no dl elements on the page.

3. If you save the file and refresh your browser, you should see the jsTrace window shown in Figure 8-5.

Note You'll be using `trace()` throughout this script so you can pause at just about any time to refresh your browser and see that everything is working as expected.

Figure 8-5. *jsTrace shows that something has transpired.*

4. All the answers are currently collapsed (that is, they're invisible because you threw them off the left side of the page). You don't want the CSS interaction and the JavaScript interaction butting heads, so you need to trigger the CSS to release its stranglehold on those answers. To do that, simply add a class to the dl to signify that the FAQ has been turned on:

```
initialize:    function(){
  trace( 'initialize()' );
  // Collect the DLs & loop
  $$( 'dl.faq' ).each( function( dl ){
    trace( 'DL loop' );
    // Turn "on" the FAQ
    dl.addClassName( 'on' );
  }.bind( this ) ); // End DL loop
},
```

5. In firebug.css just add the appropriate selector (.faq.on dd) to the declaration block you already created for .faq dd:target—and you're all set:

```
.faq.on dd,
.faq dd:target {
  position: static;
}
```

> **Note** Remember that IE 6 does not understand multiple class selectors and will default to using the last class defined in the selector (on in this case). If IE 6 is a major target for you and you think there may be conflict, you might want to use faq-on instead.

6. Since you're in the style sheet, go ahead and add the following rule:

```
.faq.on dd {
  margin-top: 0;
  padding-top: 0;
}
```

This will reset the `margin-top` and `padding-top` for the `dd` because you don't need them when FAQ is turned on.

7. Save the CSS file and refresh to view the answers fully expanded.

8. Back inside the FAQ you need to do two things: prepare the `dd` elements for opening and closing and then establish the event handler for the anchors. The `dd` bit is pretty straightforward:

```
initialize:       function(){
  trace( 'initialize()' );
  // Collect the DLs & loop
  $$( 'dl.faq' ).each( function( dl ){
    trace( 'DL loop' );
    // Turn "on" the FAQ
    dl.addClassName( 'on' );
    // Loop through the DDs
    $A( dl.getElementsByTagName( 'dd' ) ).each( function( dd ){
      // Set up the height effect (using moo.fx)
      dd.heightFX = new fx.Style(
        dd, 'height',
        { duration: 500,
          onComplete: function(){
                    this.complete( dd );
                 }.bind( this )
        }
      );
      // store the original height for later
      dd.openHeight = dd.getHeight();
      // Close this DD
      dd.heightFX.set( 0 );
    }.bind( this ) ); // End DD loop
  }.bind( this ); // End DL loop
},
```

This code collects the <dd> elements within each FAQ dl and makes them enumerable (using Prototype's $A()). It then iterates through each (using Prototype's Enumerable .each() method), setting the dd elements heightFX property to be an instance of fx.Style, which is a generic way Moo.fx enables you to transition a CSS property from one value to another (and enables you to include only the base Moo.fx library). In this example, you'll transition the height property of the dd over a period of half a second (500ms) and trigger the FAQ.complete() method (which currently doesn't do anything, but will do some housekeeping for you later on) when the effect has finished. Finally, this addition uses Prototype's Element.getHeight() method to store the current height of the dd in its openHeight property and then uses the fx.Style object's set() method to set the height of each dd to 0, thereby collapsing them.

> **Note** All the calls to bind(this) help maintain proper scope for this within the loops and the effect. Whenever this is used within this script, it refers to the FAQ object.

9. If you were to refresh the browser at this point, you'd see a terrible mess because you shrank the height of the dd, but didn't tell it to hide any of the content that overflows its box. One minor addition to the style sheet covers it:

```
.faq.on dd {
  margin-top: 0;
  padding-top: 0;
  overflow: hidden;
}
```

10. Another refresh, and everything's golden; the dd elements are collapsed and none of the content is sticking out. Now it's time to tackle those anchors.

11. Handling the anchors is not overly complex. You can loop through and collect all the anchors inside the dl and then determine whether you need to set an onclick event handler by asking whether or not the href contains an in-page id reference and whether that id actually exists (just to be sure). If you need to set the event handler, use Prototype's Event.observe() and determine whether the anchor is a question within that handler (which should close any open answers and scroll to and open its own) or a reference to another question (in which case, it should just open the new answer and scroll to it). This determination can easily be made by simply checking to see whether the link's parentNode is a dt and then triggering the appropriate FAQ method.

```
initialize:    function(){
  trace( 'initialize()' );
  // Collect the DLs & loop
  $$( 'dl.faq' ).each( function( dl ){
    ...cut...
    // Loop through the ANCHORs
    $A( dl.getElementsByTagName( 'a' ) ).each( function( a ){
      var href = a.getAttribute( 'href' );
      /* Drop out if the link is not an in-page ANCHOR
         or if it's TARGET cannot be found */
      if( !href.match( /#/ )||
          !$( href.replace( /.*?#(.*)/, '' ) ) ) return;
      // set the event handler
      Event.observe( a, 'click', function( e ){
        var el = Event.element( e );
        var id = el.getAttribute( 'href' ).replace( /.*?#/, '' );
        trace( 'looking for ' + id );
```

```
            // check to see if this link is already open
            if( this.open_items.indexOf( id ) == -1 ){
              this.to_open = id;
              // See if the ANCHOR is inside a DT
              if( el.parentNode.nodeName.toUpperCase() == 'DT' ){
                /* If yes, we need to set the action to close
                   any open FAQs and then go */
                this.closeAndGo();
              } else {
                // Otherwise we need to just go to the chosen FAQ
                this.goTo();
              }
            }
            return false;
          }.bind( this ), false );
        }.bind( this ) ); // End ANCHOR loop
      } // End DL loop
    },
```

Before you move on, let's talk about where things are wiring into one another. You're tying into two methods, FAQ.closeAndGo() and FAQ.goTo(), for handling the close-scroll-open (for a question click) and scroll-open (for a reference click) interactions, respectively. You'll fill in the logic for those methods in a moment. Keep in mind that the links won't be functional until you do.

You're also starting to make use of some of the properties of the FAQ object. The first, as you might have noticed, is FAQ.open_items. Before you execute any action in the event handler, you test to see whether the id referenced by the clicked anchor is already in that array (using Prototype's Array.indexOf()). When you get to writing the FAQ.open() method, you'll set it to add the id of the newly opened answer to FAQ.open_items.

This brings you to the second property used here: FAQ.to_open. This property enables you to track the id of the element you're opening, so you don't have to keep passing it as an argument from method to method.

Refreshing the page at this point gives you a trace of the events taking place as you click each question link. Obviously, you haven't written the code to actually open the answers back up, but the clicks are triggering the script to look for the correct id, as shown in Figure 8-6.

Figure 8-6. *A trace of some question clicks*

Opening Up

With the stage set by `FAQ.initialize()`, you can begin to work on the animation for opening and closing the dd elements. The click events trigger one of two different methods, depending on their context: `FAQ.closeAndGo()` or `FAQ.goTo()`.

1. Before getting into them, fill in `FAQ.open()`:

```
open:                function(){
  trace( 'open()' );
  var dd = $( this.to_open );
  dd.heightFX.custom( 0, dd.openHeight );
},
```

This method is pretty straightforward; it finds the dd you want to open ($(this. to_open)) and then implements a custom animation, triggering the dd height to transition from 0 to the height you stored in the dd openHeight property.

2. Next, set `FAQ.goTo()` to open the dd (you'll be adding in some scroll triggers later, but for now, keep it simple):

```
goTo:                function(){
  trace( 'goTo()' );
  this.open();
},
```

3. Add in the logic for `FAQ.closeAndGo()`:

```
closeAndGo:        function(){
  trace( 'need to close '+this.open_items.length+' dds' );
  if( this.open_items.length > 0 ){
    $A( this.open_items ).each( function( id ){
      var dd = $( id );
      dd.heightFX.custom( dd.openHeight, 0 );
    }.bind( this ) );
  }
  this.goTo();
},
```

All `FAQ.closeAndGo()` does is close any open dd elements (which it obtains by referencing `FAQ.open_items`) and then calls `FAQ.goTo()`. You have not written any logic to add anything to the `FAQ.open_items` array, however, so do that now. This is where the `FAQ.complete()` method comes in.

4. You might recall that you set the size transition effect to call `FAQ.complete()` when the effect was done, so it is the perfect place to add and remove items from the `FAQ.open_items` array. Since you'll use this method on both open *and* close, you'll pass the method a reference to the dd whose animation just completed. If its id matches `FAQ.to_open`, you know it is the newly opened dd and can add it to the `FAQ.open_items` array using `Array.push()`. If not, it has just closed, and you can remove it from the array using Prototype's `Array.without()`:

```
complete:        function( dd ){
  trace( 'transition complete' );
  var id = dd.getAttribute( 'id' );
  if( this.to_open == id ){
    this.open_items.push( id );
  } else {
    this.open_items = this.open_items.without( id );
  }
},
```

5. Save your work and refresh the browser. Upon clicking the first question, you should see it slide open. Click the second question; the first will slide shut while the second slides open. Now, click the last question; this one is a test of the referencing link event. When it opens, click the link inside; you should see the answer to the first question open, but the one you started from will not have closed, just as you planned. Clicking another question will close those two and open the new one, and so on.

■Tip If the animation looks a little choppy to you, try commenting out the `<script>` element linking to jsTrace in `faq.html`. Without the jsTrace defined, `trace()` calls will be ignored, and everything will run a little more smoothly.

Everything is progressing nicely, but before you jump into the scrolling, let's talk a little bit about conflict.

Reducing Conflict

When you have a lot of animation, scrolling, and so forth in a page, it can get a little distracting and possibly overwhelming for the user. Also, if the answers in your FAQ vary greatly in length, you can end up with some very strange scrolling behaviors as they shrink and enlarge.

It would be nice to have an orderly means of triggering events so you don't have this sort of conflict. Open questions should have time to close before the page begins to scroll, and the scrolling should come to a halt before the new question opens up.

One way of accomplishing this is to set up a process queue and instruct methods to wait their turn. You'll implement it using two helper methods and a few of the properties of the FAQ object that you already defined.

1. You'll start with FAQ.processing(). This simple method will return true if there is anything in the FAQ.processes queue and false if there isn't. It will be the indicator to a method about whether it is safe to proceed with carrying out its business:

```
processing:      function(){
  trace( 'current processes: ' + this.processes.toString() );
  return ( this.processes.length > 0 ) ? true : false;
},
```

2. `FAQ.wait()` accepts an argument of the method name that needs to wait and sets a timer to try that method again in 10ms:

```
wait:              function( method ){
  trace( 'waiting to run this.' + method + '()' );
  this.timer[ method ] = setTimeout( 'FAQ.' + method + '()', 10 );
  return false;
},
```

3. Implementation of these methods is pretty straightforward. You'll start with `FAQ.open()`:

```
open:              function(){
  if( this.processing() ) return this.wait( 'open' );
  clearTimeout( this.timer['open'] );
  trace( 'open()' );
  var dd = $( this.to_open );
  dd.heightFX.custom( 0, dd.openHeight );
},
```

When `FAQ.open()` is called, it checks to see whether there are any active processes. If there are, it waits and tries again 10ms later. Once the coast is clear, the timer (which is stored as part of the `FAQ.timer` object) gets the axe, and the script proceeds normally.

4. Take a minute and implement this for `FAQ.closeAndGo()` and `FAQ.goTo()`:

```
closeAndGo:        function(){
  if( this.processing() ) return this.wait( 'closeAndGo' );
  clearInterval( this.timer['closeAndGo'] );
  trace( 'need to close '+this.open_items.length+' dds' );
  ...cut...
},
...cut...
goTo:              function(){
  if( this.processing() ) return this.wait( 'goTo' );
  clearInterval( this.timer['goTo'] );
  trace( 'goTo()' );
  ...cut...
},
```

5. With that done, you can set up the addition and removal of the dd closing processes (you'll add the scroll ones in a minute):

```
closeAndGo:        function(){
  ...cut...
  if( this.open_items.length > 0 ){
    $A( this.open_items ).each( function( id ){
      trace( 'closing ' + id );
      this.processes.push( id );
```

```
        var dd = $( id );
        dd.heightFX.custom( dd.openHeight, 0 );
      }.bind( this ) );
    }
    this.goTo();
  },
  complete:        function( dd ){
    ...cut...
    this.processes = this.processes.without( id );
  },
```

Note You can safely skip adding the open process to the list because in this example FAQ.open() will always be the last method called.

---

6. If you save the script, refresh your browser, and click a few links, you'll see open answers close before new ones are opened. Perfect.

Now, you've got some scrollin' to do.

Getting Things Scrolling

The scrolling effect is actually quite simple and involves only a few of the methods. FAQ.getScrollLeft() and FAQ.getScrollTop(), which obtain the current scroll position, have already been provided for you, which enables you to jump right into FAQ.scroll().

1. FAQ.scroll() will handle the scrolling of the page from start to finish, and because you have FAQ.processes to tell you what's going on, this method can easily determine whether it is starting the scroll or in the midst of it. FAQ.scroll() will also be able to tell when it should stop scrolling by comparing the current scroll position (determined by using FAQ.getScrollLeft() and FAQ.getScrollTop()) to its intended destination. You'll also cache the current scroll position in FAQ.scroll_cache, so you can easily determine whether the window just won't scroll any more (that is, you are at the bottom or top of the window):

```
scroll:           function(){
  if( this.processes.indexOf( 'scroll' ) != -1 ){
    // scrolling
    var left = this.getScrollLeft();
    var top = this.getScrollTop();
    if( // damn close
       ( Math.abs( left - this.scrolling_to[0] ) <= 1 &&
         Math.abs( top - this.scrolling_to[1] ) <= 1 ) ||
       // can't scroll any farther
       ( this.scroll_cache &&
         ( this.scroll_cache[0] == left &&
           this.scroll_cache[1] == top ) ) ){
```

```
      trace( 'wrapping the scroll()' );
      window.scrollTo( this.scrolling_to[0], this.scrolling_to[1] );
      clearInterval( this.timer.scroll );
      this.scroll_cache = null;
      this.processes = this.processes.without( 'scroll' );
    } else {
      trace( 'scrolling()' );
      window.scrollTo( left + ( this.scrolling_to[0] - left )/2,
                       top + ( this.scrolling_to[1] - top )/2 );
      this.scroll_cache = [ left, top ];
    }
  } else {
    trace( 'starting the scroll()' );
    this.processes.push( 'scroll' );
    this.timer.scroll = setInterval( 'FAQ.scroll()', 100 );
  }
},
```

You define yet another timer (`FAQ.timer.scroll`) to repeatedly trigger `FAQ.scroll()` at 100ms intervals to smoothly move you down the page to the destination coordinates set in `FAQ.scrolling_to`.

2. Those coordinates are set in `FAQ.goTo()` by using another helper method, `FAQ.getDT()`, before calling `FAQ.scroll()`. `FAQ.getDT()` returns a reference to the DT associated with the dd being opened. `FAQ.goTo()` uses this reference to get the dt element's position using Prototype's `Position.cumulativeOffset()`:

```
goTo:            function(){
  ...cut...
  /* We are looking to scroll to the DT so we
     need its position */
  this.scrolling_to = Position.cumulativeOffset( this.getDT() );
  trace( 'DT position: '+ this.scrolling_to[0] + ',' + this.scrolling_to[1] );
  this.scroll();
  this.open();
},
...cut...
getDT:           function(){
  trace( 'looking for the DT associated with ' + this.to_open );
  var el = $( this.to_open ).previousSibling;
  while( el.nodeName.toLowerCase() != 'dt' ){
    el = el.previousSibling;
  }
  return el;
},
```

And because you have implemented process handling, you can safely call `FAQ.open()` from within `FAQ.goTo()` without causing conflict with the call to `FAQ.scroll()` just ahead of it. You're in the final stretch now; you just have a little cleanup left to do.

Time to Tidy Up a Bit

Because you're invoking the scroll before you open the targeted answer, you can sometimes end up with a little extra room to scroll after the answer is fully open. To compensate for this, you can set the FAQ.complete() method to attempt a little more of a scroll just in case it's available:

```
complete:        function( dd ){
  ...cut...
  if( this.to_open == id ){
    this.open_items.push( id );
    // run the scroll again (just in case the page has changed)
    this.scrolling_to = Position.cumulativeOffset( this.getDT() );
    this.scroll();
  } else {
    this.open_items = this.open_items.without( id );
  }
  this.processes = this.processes.without( id );
},
```

The final little tweak has to do with bookmarking. You want the answers to be book-markable so that the following are true:

- The bookmarked question automatically opens when the page loads.

- If someone links to a bookmark, and the person following that link doesn't have JavaScript enabled, the bookmark will work for the second user, too.

- The page won't jump to the anchor reference when it loads (because you want the script to control the scrolling if it can).

One way to meet all these needs is to do a little dynamic id rewriting and then set the script to transpose any fragment identifier found in the URI string to the new id schema and trigger the referenced dd to open. You do this so the id referenced can't be found, enabling JavaScript to control the scroll. All the logic goes into FAQ.initialize():

```
initialize:      function(){
  ...cut...
  $$( 'dl.faq' ).each( function( dl ){
    ...cut...
    $A( dl.getElementsByTagName( 'dd' ) ).each( function( dd ){
      ...cut...
      // Reset the ID (so we can keep bookmarking active)
      var new_id = 'FAQ_' + dd.getAttribute( 'id' );
      dd.setAttribute( 'id', new_id );
      // Close this DD
      dd.heightFX.set( 0 );
    }.bind( this ) ); // End DD Loop
    // Loop through the ANCHORs
    $A( dl.getElementsByTagName( 'a' ) ).each( function( a ){
      var href = a.getAttribute( 'href' );
```

```
      /* Drop out if the link is not an in-page ANCHOR
         or if it's TARGET cannot be found */
      if( !href.match( /#/ )||
          !$( href.replace( /.*?#(.*)/, "FAQ_$1" ) ) ) return;
      // set the event handler
      Event.observe( a, 'click', function( e ){
        var el = Event.element( e );
        var id = 'FAQ_' + el.getAttribute( 'href' ).replace( /.*?#/, '' );
        ...cut...
      }.bind( this ), false );
    }.bind( this ) ); // End ANCHOR loop
  }.bind( this ) ); // End DL loop
  // See if we have a bookmark situation
  if( window.location.toString().indexOf( '#' ) != -1 ){
    var id = 'FAQ_' + window.location.hash.toString().replace( /#/, '' );
    trace( 'loading with bookmark: ' + id );
    if( !$( id ) ){
      trace( "can't find " + id );
    } else {
      this.to_open = id;
      this.open();
    }
  }
},
```

The first change is to rewrite the id of the dd in the dd loop. Then, in the anchor loop, you make sure that it does the transposition of the id referenced in the anchor (that is, the original one) to the newly created id ('FAQ_' + the original one). This keeps everything working nicely in the script's normal operations.

The final step is to add the handler for an id reference existing in the URI (that is, an answer that has been bookmarked or directly linked to). You transpose the fragment identifier into the new id schema and then test its existence. If it exists, you open it. Easy, peasy.

Save your work, refresh your browser, and take a look. There you have it: a beautiful, progressively enhanced FAQ.

Summary

This case study walked you through the creation of a progressively enhanced FAQ interface. The baseline was a semantically marked-up list of questions and answers (using a definition list). The next level of experience involved the use of some advanced CSS to spice things up a little bit, showing and hiding content in an accessible way using the :target pseudoclass selector. The final level of experience was delivered via JavaScript, which dynamically opened and closed the answers with a nice sliding motion and scrolled the page to make reading easier.

In addition to learning the techniques needed to accomplish this task, you also got to work a little more with the Prototype and Moo.fx libraries, and you learned how to manage potential script conflicts by keeping track of processes.

CHAPTER 9

A Dynamic Help System

By Dan Webb

Modern web applications are often characterized as having richer and more dynamic interfaces that mimic the desktop experiences much more closely than their predecessors. Most of the credit for this can be given to the major JavaScript libraries (and, of course, to their developers) as we now have a much more solid base on which to work when starting to develop these interfaces. JavaScript libraries, as discussed throughout this book, take care of lots of the detail of cross-browser compatibility and JavaScript's quirks. When writing a web application, however, they are rarely the only challenges you'll face. Your user interface (UI) must interact with server-side code well, be as robust as possible (even on platforms that don't support JavaScript (JS), and be easily maintainable.

To this end, this project illustrates implementing a typical dynamic UI feature, from planning and design right through to interfacing with server-side elements, to give you a good idea of how to write solid JavaScript in the context of a real application. In this case, you'll implement a help feature.

The code examples in this chapter are based on Ruby On Rails, the web development framework *du jour*, for your code examples. I chose it because it works well with your chosen JavaScript libraries, Prototype and Low Pro, and because it has a knack for doing its job without getting in the way of the real meat of the project—in this case, HTML, Cascading Style Sheets (CSS), JavaScript, and the concept of progressive enhancement. However, if you're not familiar with Ruby On Rails, don't worry. The concepts shown in the code examples can easily be reimplemented in PHP, Java, Django, or whatever other kind of crazy platform takes your fancy.

The Job at Hand

So what exactly will you be creating? Well, let's set the scene a little. After any application, web-based or not, has a nontrivial feature set, it will need some kind of help system to guide users around the application and provide supporting information. Many web applications tackle this problem by having a help link that typically pops up a new browser window with the help content inside. Users then scrabble around trying to find the information relative to the part of the application they're using at the time and then proceed to enter into a frustrating window-shuffling dance in which they try to refer to the help and the application at the same time. Not ideal.

However, many desktop applications have had a better solution than this for some time: the Talking Paper Clip. Well, maybe not. Joking aside, what I'm actually referring to here is the contextual help sidebar that can be seen in applications such as Microsoft Word and Excel, as well as in many other common applications. When users need help with a certain part of the application, they can press a key combination or click a help button or icon and then be shown the relevant part of the help alongside the application they are working with—no hunting for the correct help section or shuffling between the help window and the application window necessary. The help you want is given to you where you need it.

This project will take this feature from the desktop to web applications using a little Ajax and a sprinkle of server-side magic. So without further ado, let's get on with it.

Planning and Preparation

Besides regular preparation work, such as creating files and downloading library code (which will be covered later on), it is worth doing some planning for the project up front. No diagrams or written specs are required; simply pause before you start bashing away at the keyboard and think about how the project will go together.

To provide the most robust implementation you'll provide the help sidebar as a progressive enhancement to the regular help system. This means that you'll build the plain HTML and CSS nondynamic version of the feature and ensure that it works before enhancing the UI with the help sidebar using document object model (DOM) scripting. This way you can ensure that users can get access to help if their browser doesn't support JavaScript or their firewall blocks JavaScript, albeit in a more basic fashion. The bottom line is that the help content should be accessible in as many cases as possible, instead of not being available unless you have a modern JavaScript-capable browser.

There's a certain amount of forward planning required in providing good progressive enhancement. Take a leaf from Jeremy Keith's book: plan for progressive enhancement from the start; implement at the end. Although you'll build the basic application first and then layer on the help sidebar as an enhancement, it pays to plan for this right from the start. After you write progressive enhancements once or twice it becomes habit, but for now outline your plan of how to implement the feature.

The Master Plan

Planning a progressively enhanced feature is all about setting out the flow of the basic version of the feature and then identifying at what points your progressive enhancement diverges from it (see Figure 9-1).

As you can see, the basic and enhanced versions of the feature differ very little in terms of application flow. Perfect. When you work with progressive enhancement, this is a sign that your design is good. If you find that you're writing two totally separate applications for browsers with and without JavaScript, it's worth having a major rethink. There's normally a better way.

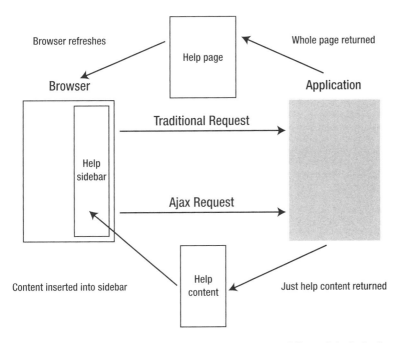

Figure 9-1. *A diagram showing the basic and enhanced flow of the help feature*

Preparing the Project

I assume that you have Ruby and Ruby On Rails installed on your machine. If you don't, you can visit the Ruby On Rails site to get full instructions on its installation (`http://rubyonrails.org/download`). After you have Rails installed, download the example code from `www.apress.com` and unzip it to your working directory (I also listed it at the end of this chapter for quick reference). This gives you a Rails application with some of the donkey work done for you so you can concentrate on the UI.

The only files you'll need to manipulate are those in the public directory (which contains the style sheets and scripts) and those in `app/views` (the HTML templates, with `.rhtml` extensions). Notice that the library files you'll use are placed in `public/javascripts`. In this project you'll use Prototype (`prototype.js`), Low Pro (`lowpro.js`), and finally, for visual effects, Moo.fx for Prototype (`moofx.js`). You'll be taking a closer look at these later—now you can start writing some HTML.

Writing the Markup

Although this is not a book about HTML, it's worth stressing that writing the HTML for an application should be a considered process instead of an afterthought. The HTML is the foundation of your UI in any web application, so careful and semantic use of HTML and considered use of IDs and classes will really help you when it comes to DOM scripting.

Really think about whether you're using the correct elements for the content in hand and be careful not to fall into the trap of "divitis" (wrapping everything in `<div>` elements and bloating out your HTML). A nice, clean, and meaningful markup means that, in many cases, browsers can do much of your work for you. Use `<a>` tags to link to content, `<ul>` and `<ol>` to mark up lists and forms, and buttons to trigger server-side actions. Work with the grain of the browser instead of misusing elements and then coding around your misuse with JavaScript. With that said, let's get into the code.

Using Layouts for Common Markup

First you need to write the common HTML that will form the layout of your application. In Ruby On Rails terms, a *layout* is a means of including common elements in many pages of your application. You can think of it as the inverse of server-side includes (such as those supported by many platforms such as PHP and ASP). Instead of defining snippets of common content that are included into each of your documents, a layout is a common template into which page-specific content is injected (see Figure 9-2).

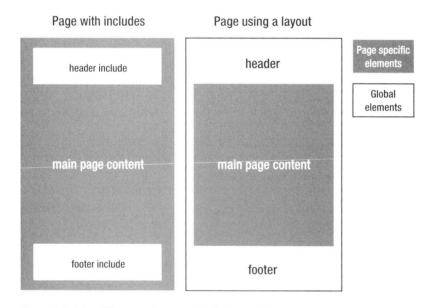

Figure 9-2. *The differences between includes and layouts*

Although layouts are a Ruby On Rails feature, many other frameworks, including CakePHP, CodeIgniter, and Django, have an equivalent. Even if your platform doesn't, you can roll your own rather simply. As you'll see, as well as being a generally useful tool, layouts will also become very useful to you later on down the line.

Following is the layout you'll be starting with for your application:

```
<!DOCTYPE html PUBLIC "-//W3C//DTD XHTML 1.0 Strict//EN"
  "http://www.w3.org/TR/xhtml1/DTD/xhtml1-strict.dtd">
<html>
  <head>
    <meta http-equiv="Content-type" content="text/html; charset=utf-8">
    <title>Pro DOM Scripting with Ajax, APIs and Libraries Chapter 9</title>
  </head>

  <body>
    <div id="content">
      <div id="header">
        <h1>Examplr Beta</h1>
      </div>

      <%= yield %>

    </div>
  </body>
</html>
```

In Rails, the `<%= yield %>` statement marks where each page's content will be inserted into the layout. This simple layout includes a content area (the `<div>` with the id content) with an application-wide header. You'll add an area for the help sidebar content later in the "Styling with CSS" section.

This file can be found at app/views/layouts/application.rhtml in the example application.

Adding an Example Application Page

With the layout in place, you can turn your attention to the application pages themselves. For the sake of this project you'll create only one application page, the suitably confusing Add A Sprocket form. Users are bound to need some help with this.

Once again, the markup is simple:

```
<h2>Add A Sprocket <a href="/help/sprocket" rel="help">?</a></h2>

<form action="/nowhere" method="post">
  <fieldset>
    <p><label for="name">Name</label> <input name="name" id="name" /></p>
    <p><label for="spid">Sprocket ID <a href="/help/sprocket#sprocketid"
rel="help">?</a></label> <input name="spid" id="spid" /></p>
    <p><label for="desc">Description</label> <textarea name="desc"
id="desc"></textarea></p>
    <p><label for="tr">Tacion Rating <a href="/help/tacion"
rel="help">?</a></label> <input name="tr" id="tr" /></p>
    <p class="check"><label for="xx75">XX-75 Approved <a href="/help/xx75"
```

```
rel="help">?</a></label> <input name="xx75" id="xx75" type="checkbox" /></p>
    <p class="submit"><input type="submit" name="submit"
        value="Add Sprocket" /></p>
  </fieldset>
</form>
```

You can find this file at app/views/main/index.rhtml in the example application. Notice that contextual help links are added with a rel attribute of "help" throughout the form. The rel attribute describes the relationship of the link to the resource and is a very convenient hook for many types of scripts. Later you'll use the rel attribute to determine whether the resulting content in the help sidebar should display when a link is clicked. You could also use a class name to differentiate help links from other normal links on the page, but in this case it seems most semantically correct to specify a relationship.

These links point to various pages within the help section. In the example code the help section is hooked up for you, but it's worth having a brief look at the controller code:

```
class HelpController < ApplicationController

  def show
    render :template => '/help/' + params[:path].join('/'), :layout => 'help'
  end

end
```

For those not familiar with Rails or Ruby, this action renders the specified template from within app/views/help with the layout named help. For instance, the URL /help/sprocket will render the template at app/views/help/sprocket.rhtml. (I put a few example help pages in there for you.) The help layout looks fairly similar to the main page layout. Try clicking one of the help links and you'll see the result: the help content is rendered in its own page.

You have achieved your first goal: you have a form with working links to your help content. Now it's time to start the progressive enhancement and layer on the help sidebar behavior.

Styling with CSS

This is a book about JavaScript, not CSS, so I won't get into too much detail about styling the form. For this example, use the CSS file included in the example files (public/stylesheets/main.css). To use this CSS file in your Rails project, open the layout file (app/views/layouts/application.rhtml) and insert this line into the <head> of the document:

```
<%= stylesheet_link_tag "main" %>
```

You should now have a styled form page. At this point you need to think about the help panel and how it will be styled. First you'll need to add the help panel into the HTML. Add a <div id="help"> to your layout. You can add a little bit of fake content in there temporarily for testing if you need to. Here's how the layout looks now:

```
<!DOCTYPE html PUBLIC "-//W3C//DTD XHTML 1.0 Strict//EN"
  "http://www.w3.org/TR/xhtml1/DTD/xhtml1-strict.dtd">
<html>
  <head>
    <meta http-equiv="Content-type" content="text/html; charset=utf-8">
    <title>Pro DOM Scripting with Ajax, APIs and Libraries Chapter 9</title>
    <%= stylesheet_link_tag "main" %>
  </head>

  <body>
    <div id="content">
      <div id="header">
        <h1>Examplr Beta</h1>
      </div>

      <%= yield %>

    </div>
    <div id="help">
      Some example help content.
    </div>
  </body>
</html>
```

You'll notice that the help panel is now on the page, but it is dangling at the end of the form in a rather ugly way. You can use CSS to rectify this. The help panel will have two states: closed (which is the default) and open. When closed, you simply need to hide the panel altogether. To this end, add this style rule to your CSS:

```
#help {
  display: none;
}
```

When the panel is open the main panel needs to make space on the right for the panel, and the panel needs to be shown in that space. You could do this by manipulating the element's style property with JavaScript, but it's much better to use the right tool for the right job. CSS is for presentation, so you can use a class on the body to denote whether the page has help open or closed. If the body of the document has the class name with-help you can apply the relevant styles to show the help panel. Add the following to the CSS:

```
body.with-help {
  margin-right: 350px;
}
```

```
body.with-help #help {
  background: #F4EEBC;
  border: 1px solid #000;
  border-color: #CCC #333 #333 #CCC;
  width: 320px;
  position: absolute;
  top: 0;
  right: 0;
  margin: 8px 30px;
  padding: 10px;
  overflow: hidden;
}
```

If you have Firebug installed in your browser you can test the open and closed states by opening the console and typing the following:

```
document.body.className = "with-help";
```

Enter Prototype and Low Pro

Prototype was the first of the current generation of JavaScript libraries that are powering many of the latest applications on the Web. Prototype (for which you can find downloads and full documentation at `http://prototypejs.org`) is now shipped with Ruby On Rails, but it can be (and is) regularly used on its own. Scriptaculous is commonly used with it to provide effects and components. But because you'll be using only lightweight effects in this application, the smaller and simpler Moo.fx library will be most appropriate.

Finally, because you'll code this feature in an unobtrusive style you'll need a few extra utilities that are contained in the Low Pro (`http://danwebb.net/lowpro`) library, another extension library to Prototype. Low Pro contains a whole raft of useful extensions to Prototype's event handling, DOM manipulation and creation, and something that you'll be using heavily in this application: behaviors.

I'll discuss the parts of these libraries that you need as you use them, so don't worry if you're not familiar with them at this point—you will be by the end of the chapter. It is, however, a good idea to have a browser tab open with the Prototype API documentation in it (you can find it at `http://prototypejs.org/api/`).

Using the Libraries in Your Project

Prototype, Low Pro, and Moo.fx are all included in the example files. To add them into your project, open the `application.rhtml` layout file and add the following into the head of the document:

```
<%= javascript_include_tag 'prototype', 'lowpro', 'moofx' %>
```

Or, of course, you can write the HTML directly:

```
<script type="text/javascript" src="/javascripts/prototype.js"></script>
<script type="text/javascript" src="/javascripts/lowpro.js"></script>
<script type="text/javascript" src="/javascripts/moofx.js"></script>
```

With that you're ready to bring your help sidebar to life.

Bringing Help to Life

As they say on MTV *Cribs*, this is where the magic happens. Now you need to add the JavaScript behavior layer that will turn your basic help system into a dynamic contextual sidebar. There is, in fact, very little JavaScript required to get you off the ground, which is indicative of a solid design. If you let all the other parts of the application handle the jobs, they should; then JavaScript just needs to be the behavioral glue to connect events on the page to actions.

Building the Help Controller

To help you manage the code you need to implement the help sidebar and wrap it up in an object. Because there is only one help sidebar per page, you can represent the help with a single Help object. Open up public/javascripts/application.js to start writing the help controller. You'll start with the basic open and close functionality:

```
var Help = {
  open : function() {
    $(document.body).addClassName('with-help');
  },
  close : function() {
    $(document.body).removeClassName('with-help');
  }
};
```

As mentioned before, to open and close the sidebar you simply need to add and remove the with-help class on the body. Next you need to add a method that requests the help page via an Ajax request and updates the help element with the content. Prototype's Ajax.Updater (as discussed in Chapter 5) does exactly this:

```
Help = {
  open : function() {
    $(document.body).addClassName('with-help');
  },
  close : function() {
    $(document.body).removeClassName('with-help');
  },
```

```
  request : function(url, callback) {
    new Ajax.Updater('help', url, {
      method: 'get',
      onComplete: callback.bind(this)
    });
  }

};
```

The new request() method takes a URL and a callback function, which will be called when the Ajax request has completed successfully. The body of the function contains an Ajax.Updater call, which updates the contents of the element with ID help, which in this case is the help sidebar, and specifies that the passed callback should be executed on completion. Notice that you're using Prototype's bind() method to ensure that the this keyword will point to the Help controller object within the callback.

When you click a help link you want to trigger the request to get a certain URL. And when the request has got the help content, you want to reveal the sidebar. So let's wrap that up in another controller method:

```
Help = {
  openWith : function(url) {
    this.request(url, function() {
      if ($(document.body).hasClassName('with-help') == false) this.open();
    });
  },
  open : function() {
    $(document.body).addClassName('with-help');
  },
  close : function() {
    $(document.body).removeClassName('with-help');
  },
  request : function(url, callback) {
    new Ajax.Updater('help', url, {
      method: 'get',
      onComplete: callback.bind(this)
    });
  }
};
```

The new openWith() method does exactly this, so now the skeleton controller object is essentially complete. The next step is to wire it to the help links on the page, which is where Low Pro comes in very handy.

Adding Behaviors

You can think of LowPro's Event.addBehavior() method as the equivalent of CSS, but for behavior instead of style (a behavior sheet, if you like). In fact, the Event.addBehavior() usage feels very similar to CSS in that it uses an extended form of CSS selectors to select elements and events to apply behavior to. A typical call might look like this:

```
Event.addBehavior({
  'a.product:click' : function() {
    // when a elements with the class 'product' are clicked
    // the code within this function will run
  },
  'div.description:mouseover' : function() {
    // when divs with the class 'description' are moused over
    // this function will run
  }
});
```

You can call Event.addBehavior() as many times as you like and it will stack the behaviors onto the elements automatically. Also, by default it will try to reapply its behaviors after every Ajax request to ensure that any new content will have the behaviors applied to it. To hook up the help controller to the help links on the page, place this in application.js:

```
Event.addBehavior({
  'a[rel=help]:click' : function() {
    Help.openWith(this.href);
    return false;
  }
});
```

Here you're using an attribute selector to select all the <a> elements with a rel attribute of help and triggering Help.openWith(), passing the link's href when it is clicked. As with normal event handlers, returning false will stop the default action of the link so you don't get taken off to the help page.

You're now ready to test it, so let's include application.js in the page by updating the application layout:

```
<%= javascript_include_tag 'prototype', 'lowpro', 'moofx', 'application' %>
```

When clicking any of the help links, you should now get the help content in the sidebar—but you aren't quite there yet. At the moment, the help content comes with a whole HTML page wrapped around it, but you just want to inject the inner content. To implement this you need to return to the Rails help controller (app/controllers/help_controller.rb) and adjust it so that if the page is requested via Ajax, you return the content with a different layout:

```
class HelpController < ApplicationController

  def show
    template = '/help/' + params[:path].join('/')
    if request.xhr?
      render :template => template, :layout => 'help_sidebar'
    else
      render :template => template, :layout => 'help'
    end
  end

end
```

You've added a condition to test whether the request does come from XMLHttpRequest (a.k.a. Ajax) and then send the same template, but with the help_sidebar layout instead. In Rails, as demonstrated previously, you can use request.xhr? to find out whether the request came via Ajax, but it's easily replicated if you aren't using Rails. Under the hood, the request.xhr? method simply checks whether the X-Requested-With HTTP header is 'XMLHttpRequest'. Prototype's Ajax routines append this header to all Ajax requests by default.

The help_sidebar layout is pretty simple. You'll notice that it doesn't contain a whole HTML document; it's just a fragment, which is what you need if you want to update just part of an existing page. You also need to add a close link that can used to close the sidebar:

```
<p id="close_help"><a href="">X</a></p>

<%= yield %>
```

Test the page again and you'll see a much better effect. The layout now remains intact when the sidebar is open. You need to make the close button work by adding another rule to the Event.addBehavior() block:

```
Event.addBehavior({
  'a[rel=help]:click' : function() {
    Help.openWith(this.href);
    return false;
  },
  '#close_help a:click' : function() {
    Help.close();
    return false;
  }
});
```

Implementing a Loader

Although the feature is now working, it's always a good idea to implement a loader to give the user some feedback if the help content is taking some time to load. A nice simple approach to this is to create a global loader that responds to all Ajax requests automatically. Fortunately, Prototype makes this really simple.

There will be only one global loader on the page, so you can represent it with a singleton object, which (boringly) will be called Loader. Loader needs to encapsulate three basic functions: initializing (which includes creating the loader element itself), showing the loader, and hiding the loader:

```
Loader = {
  initialize: function(parent) {
    this.loader =
      $img({ src: 'images/loader.gif', alt: 'Loading...', id: 'loader' });
    parent.appendChild(this.loader);
    this.hide();
```

```
  Ajax.Responders.register({
    onCreate: function() {
      Loader.show();
    },
    onComplete: function() {
      Loader.hide();
    }
  });
},
show: function() {
  this.loader.show();
},
hide: function() {
  this.loader.hide();
}
};
```

Most of the work is in the `initialize()` method. First, the method creates the loader element itself with Low Pro's DOM builder, which provides a shortcut and some cross-browser fixes for creating DOM node structures. For each HTML tag there is a $xxx() function that will create that node. If you pass in an object literal as the first argument, the given properties will be set as attributes on the element. Any other arguments are appended as children to the created node. The preceding example just creates a single <img> tag, but take a look at the following example to get an idea of how a larger node structure might go together:

```
var product = $div({ 'class' : 'product' },
  $h2('Sprocket 47'),
  $p({ 'class' : 'description' }, 'The worlds best sprocket'),
  $a({ href : '/sprockets/74'}, 'Read more')
);
```

Back to the `Loader`; after creating the loader image element, append it onto the passed parent-child nodes. The second part of the `initialize()` method then uses Prototype's `Ajax.Responders` to show and hide the loader graphic when necessary. `Ajax.Responders.register()` enables you to register global event handlers that are called whenever any Ajax call is initiated or completed. This gives you an excellent and extremely simple method by which to implement a global loader.

Now that you've finished writing the loader you need to attach it into the page. You can do this by using `Event.addBehavior()` once again:

```
Event.addBehavior({
  '#header' : function() {
    Loader.initialize(this);
  }
});
```

Here `Event.addBehavior()` is used in a slightly different way. When you just specify a CSS selector without the event type, the given function is executed as soon as the DOM is loaded. You exploit this behavior to initialize the `Loader` object passing it, which refers to the selected element, as the parent node to the loader. I added a little CSS in the `main.css` to make sure that it appears in the top-right corner of the header; then you're done.

When using Low Pro, `Event.addBehavior()` becomes the glue between the HTML document and the core JavaScript code. Decoupling JavaScript logic from the document has powerful advantages for maintainance and if the HTML changes at any point. Instead of searching through the core code to find out which code affects which element, you just change the CSS selectors to reflect the new structure of the document.

Finishing Touches

You're now pretty much done implementing the help sidebar, but there are always a few things you can do to make things a bit slicker. So to polish the feature a little bit you'll be adding some animation and a few extra features.

Adding Animation with Moo.fx

Earlier in the chapter I briefly mentioned Moo.fx, the ultra-compact effects library. Now it's time to put it into action. Let's make the help sidebar slide in and out instead of snapping straight from one state to another.

At its most basic level, animation in JavaScript is all about manipulating one or more style properties of an element over time. Moo.fx gives you a basic yet versatile interface to do this with the `fx.Style` constructor, but first you need to look at the CSS to identify what style properties you need to animate to get the sliding effect. Here are the rules in question:

```
body.with-help {
  margin-right: 350px;
}

body.with-help #help {
  background: #F4EEBC;
  border: 1px solid #000;
  border-color: #CCC #333 #333 #CCC;
  width: 320px;
  position: absolute;
  top: 0;
  right: 0;
  margin: 8px 30px;
  padding: 10px;
  overflow: hidden;
}
```

A quick look at this code tells you that the `margin-right` property needs to be animated out to 350px to make room for the help sidebar. At the same time you need to animate the `width` property of the sidebar from 0 to 320px to give the effect of it opening out. Of course, the reverse is required to close the sidebar again. You also still need to ensure that the with-help class name is added and removed as before.

Returning to application.js, you now need to create the effects objects that you can use to perform the animations. You can keep the effects you need inside the fx property of the Help object and you need to create them only once—as soon as the DOM is available. To do this, use Low Pro's Event.onReady() method:

```
Event.onReady(function() {
  Help.fx = {
    openHelp: new fx.Style('help', 'width', {
      onStart : function() {
        $(document.body).addClassName('with-help');
      }
    }),
    closeHelp: new fx.Style('help', 'width', {
      onComplete : function() {
        $(document.body).removeClassName('with-help');
      }
    }),
    slideBody: new fx.Style(document.body, 'margin-right')
  };
});
```

Here three effects are defined. First is openHelp, which operates on the width property of the help element—the sidebar. You use the onStart callback of the effect to add with-help. Second, closeHelp is very similar, but you use onComplete to remove with-help when the effect has finished. Finally, you define slideBody, which operates on the margin-right property of the document.body. Now update the open and close methods to use these effects:

```
Help = {
  SIDEBAR_WIDTH: 350,
  SIDEBAR_MARGIN: 30,
  openWith : function(url) {
    this.request(url, function() {
      if ($(document.body).hasClassName('with-help') == false) this.open();
    });
  },
  open : function() {
    Help.fx.openHelp.custom(0, this.SIDEBAR_WIDTH - this.SIDEBAR_MARGIN);
    Help.fx.slideBody.custom(this.SIDEBAR_MARGIN , this.SIDEBAR_WIDTH);
  },
  close : function() {
    Help.fx.closeHelp.custom(this.SIDEBAR_WIDTH - this.SIDEBAR_MARGIN , 0);
    Help.fx.slideBody.custom(this.SIDEBAR_WIDTH , this.SIDEBAR_MARGIN );
  },
```

```
  request : function(url, callback) {
    new Ajax.Updater('help', url, {
      method: 'get',
      onComplete: callback.bind(this)
    });
  }
};
```

Now open and close: use the custom method of the effects objects to perform the animations passing in the start and end values for the animation.

Implementing Anchors Within the Sidebar

You might have noticed that when using the basic HTML-only version of the help system, clicking the help for Sprocket ID will take you directly to that section of the sprocket help page. This is because you've used a normal HTML page anchor to ensure that the browser scrolls to the relevant section:

```
<a href="/help/sprocket#sprocketid" rel="help">?</a>
```

But after you implemented the enhanced version, which hijacks the browser's normal behavior, you lost this effect. However, it would be great to enhance the script so that users would be taken straight to the relevant part of the help in the sidebar. Maybe you could even improve on this by implementing some kind of highlighting of that section to draw the user's eye.

A great approach to solving many DOM scripting problems is to try to use the information contained within the HTML as much as possible. You previously used the href attribute of help links to inform the help system of what content to load. To implement this feature, you can examine the href attributes further to pull out the anchor portion of the href. This will give you the ID of the section you need to scroll to. You'll need to update the openWith() method of the Help object:

```
Help = {
  openWith : function(url) {
    var urlParts = url.split('#');
    var path = urlParts[0], anchor = urlParts[1];

    this.request(url, function() {
      if ($(document.body).hasClassName('with-help') == false) this.open();

      if (anchor && anchorEl = $(anchor)) {
        anchorEl.scrollTo();
        anchorEl.addClassName('highlighted');
      }
    });
  },
  ...
```

First, you split out the path and anchor portions of the URL using `split()`. Once you have the anchor portion of the URL you can initiate a request for the page as normal, but this time the callback is slightly different. If there is an anchor, and that element exists, you can use Prototype's `scrollTo()` method to scroll the browser window down to the relevant section. It very closely mimics the browser's default behavior for anchors. Finally, you add the highlighted class name on to that element, which enables you to apply some extra styles to the anchored element.

Looking Back

In this chapter you've seen that with the power of Prototype and Low Pro, and a little bit of help from Rails, you achieved quite a lot with a minimal amount of complexity. So let's take a look back over the decisions made during the implementation of the help sidebar and examine the advantage of each in more detail.

Begin with a Solid Base of Semantic HTML

JavaScript gives you almost ultimate power to manipulate the look, feel, and behavior of HTML elements, which often leads to JavaScript programmers diving straight in to scripting, writing HTML to support their script. However, if you start by thinking how to best represent the information on the page with static HTML you can take advantage of the built-in behaviors that the browser gives you, enabling you to write less code as well as ensuring that the application works as well as possible for users without JavaScript.

As a general rule, it's always advisable to start out by making a working version of your feature with static HTML. Don't worry so much about this being usable or slick. Just make it work and make sure that you put as much semantic value into the HTML as possible because the richer your content is from a semantic point of view, the more hooks you'll have available to you for your script.

In this chapter, you made sure that the static HTML version was working before even starting to write JavaScript at all. This provides a very solid foundation to build on top of, which ensures that the help content is accessible, search-engine indexable, printable, and bookmarkable. Once this is in place you can go about writing the JavaScript as an enhancement to this already fully operational feature. This is a prime example of progressive enhancement.

Using HTML, CSS, and JavaScript Appropriately

HTML is for content and structure, CSS is for presentation, and JavaScript (in the context of the browser) is for interactivity. They were each designed for their specific purpose and are the best at their particular job. It's very common, however, for developers to get into the habit of letting HTML do some of the presentation (with `<strong>`, for example, just because you want something bold, in-line style attributes, and so on) or even letting CSS do some of the inter-activity (a big example being CSS-only drop-down menus), but the biggest temptation lies within JavaScript.

JavaScript has a special role in the browser in that it has the power to manipulate presentation and content very easily. Even though this is the case, it's still normally advantageous to avoid manipulating style properties or adding content to the page. If you want to change the visual state of an element from JavaScript, do so by adding a class name (as you did using the `with-help` class earlier). Similarly, instead of generating lots of HTML from a script, ensure that it is in the document to begin with. The only common exception is animation, which necessarily manipulates the values of style properties over time.

One main advantage of working this way is that it enables you to change the look and feel of the application without going anywhere near the JavaScript itself. If the highlighted state of the selected section needs to be changed you can simply point the designer at the highlighted style rules in the CSS. Similarly, if all the content is in the HTML, a nontechnical team member can make changes to copy without going near the JavaScript. Finally, if all the content is with HTML, you can ensure that the user still has access to that content, even if JavaScript is not working.

Using CSS Selectors As Application Glue

CSS selectors are incredibly good at their job of selecting elements to apply style properties to in CSS, and now all the major JavaScript libraries have really solid implementations that are becoming faster and faster all the time, as well as supporting more of the CSS standard than the built-in browser versions. This means that CSS selectors can now not only be used to glue style to your documents but also to glue JavaScript behavior. Low Pro behaviors are one of several frameworks that automate this process, giving you what is essentially a style sheet for behavior.

The main advantage of attaching JavaScript in this way is that you can decouple your application code from the document itself. In this project, for example, you used LowPro to wire a call to `Help.openWith()` (from the application code) to links with `rel="help"`. If you want to change it (to use `class="help"` instead, for instance), it's very easy to change. In fact, it can be so simple that designers in your team can update it. The help sidebar feature is very simple, but with large projects the gains in maintainability become even more apparent. You can separate a very complex JavaScript project up into several behaviors that are then glued into the document via `Event.addBehavior()`. If the HTML structure changes, it's trivial to adapt your scripts.

When It Comes to Ajax, Simple Is Best

There are many methods of communication between JavaScript and the server side. Of course, originally, there was the *X* in Ajax: XML. Since then JSON, RJS, and plain HTML have emerged as other formats, as well as a whole raft of more niche technologies. The rule of thumb here is to go for the simplest method possible to get the job done. In most cases you don't even need anything as rich as JSON; most of the time you can just send a request, return a chunk of update HTML and replace the relevant part of the document with it. Prototype's `Ajax.Updater` makes this method extremely simple.

In this project, `Ajax.Updater` is used to great effect. There's no need to wrap the Ajax responses up in JSON and then write code to unpack it and handle it on the client side, so the returned HTML is simply placed into the sidebar `<div>`.

There are numerous advantages to keeping your Ajax communications simple. Because each user needs to download and execute the JavaScript code on each computer, less code is always best. Why write lots of code to unpack an XML or a JSON response and act on it when you can just move chunks of HTML around? Second, browser JavaScript, by its very nature, is a slow and unreliable beast. The less work you can get away with, the more likely it is to work, and the more responsive your application will be. There are, of course, many use cases in which JSON or XML might be necessary, but on the whole you can get away with something very simple—so always strive for that.

Summary

In implementing the sidebar feature in this chapter I hopefully demonstrated that progressive enhancement is no more difficult than old-fashioned, obtrusive scripting. Especially with tools such as Low Pro, you can get powerful results without the expense of breaking browser functionality, rendering your application inaccessible or useless to users on mobile browsers or behind firewalls. There's a common misconception that progressive enhancement is more effort than obtrusive techniques, and even that progressive enhancement is not possible for most applications, but I'm sure you'll find that this is simply not the case. Progressive enhancement should be your default approach to DOM scripting.

Source Code

Rails generates a large amount of boilerplate code to support your application, but for this project only a few files are actually relevant. Following are the complete listings of those files for your reference.

Listing 9-1. *The application layout (*app/views/layouts/application.rhtml*)*

```
<!DOCTYPE html PUBLIC "-//W3C//DTD XHTML 1.0 Strict//EN"
  "http://www.w3.org/TR/xhtml1/DTD/xhtml1-strict.dtd">
<html>
  <head>
    <meta http-equiv="Content-type" content="text/html; charset=utf-8">
    <title>Pro DOM Scripting with Ajax, APIs and Libraries Chapter 9</title>
    <%= stylesheet_link_tag 'main' %>
    <%= javascript_include_tag 'prototype', 'lowpro', 'moofx', 'application' %>
  </head>

  <body>
    <div id="content">
      <div id="header">
        <h1>Examplr Beta</h1>
      </div>

      <%= yield %>
```

```
      </div>

      <div id="help"></div>
    </body>
</html>
```

Listing 9-2. *The full page help layout* (app/views/layouts/help.rhtml)

```
<!DOCTYPE html PUBLIC "-//W3C//DTD XHTML 1.0 Strict//EN"
  "http://www.w3.org/TR/xhtml1/DTD/xhtml1-strict.dtd">
<html>
  <head>
    <meta http-equiv="Content-type" content="text/html; charset=utf-8">
    <title>Pro DOM Scripting with Ajax, APIs and Libraries Chapter 9</title>
    <%= stylesheet_link_tag 'main' %>
  </head>

  <body>
    <div id="content">
      <div id="header">
        <h1>Examplr Help</h1>
      </div>

    <%= yield %>

    </div>
  </body>
</html>
```

Listing 9-3. *The help sidebar layout* (app/views/layouts/help_sidebar.rhtml)

```
<p id="close_help"><a href="">X</a></p>

<%= yield %>
```

Listing 9-4. *The form page* (app/views/main/index.rhtml)

```
<h2>Add A Sprocket <a href="/help/sprocket" rel="help">?</a></h2>

<form action="/nowhere" method="post">
  <fieldset>
    <p><label for="name">Name</label> <input name="name" id="name" /></p>
    <p><label for="spid">Sprocket ID <a href="/help/sprocket#sprocketid"
rel="help">?</a></label> <input name="spid" id="spid" /></p>
    <p><label for="desc">Description</label> <textarea name="desc"
id="desc"></textarea></p>
    <p><label for="tr">Tacion Rating <a href="/help/tacion"
```

```
rel="help">?</a></label> <input name="tr" id="tr" /></p>
    <p class="check"><label for="xx75">XX-75 Approved <a href="/help/xx75"
rel="help">?</a></label> <input name="xx75" id="xx75" type="checkbox" /></p>
    <p class="submit"><input type="submit" name="submit" value="Add Sprocket"
/></p>
  </fieldset>
</form>
```

Listing 9-5. *The application CSS file* (public/stylesheets/main.css)

```css
body {
  background: #999;
  padding: 0 30px;
  font-family: helvetica, arial, sans-serif;
}

#content {
  background: #FFF;
  border: 1px solid #FFF;
  border-color: #CCC #333 #333 #CCC;
}

#header {
  background: #5D8ED3;
  padding: 1em;
  color: #FFF;
  font-family: georgia, serif;
  position: relative;
}

#content h2, #content form, #content p, #content h3 {
  margin: 1em 1em;
}

fieldset {
  border: 0;
  width: 50%;
}

#content h2 {
  font-family: georgia, serif;
  border-bottom: 1px solid #5D8ED3;
  padding-bottom: 0.5em;
}
```

```
label {
  display: block;
}

input, textarea {
  width: 99%;
}

textarea {
  height: 7em;
}

p.check label {
  display: inline;
}

p.check input, p.submit input {
  width: auto;
}

fieldset p {
  padding: 0.7em 0;
  margin: 1px;
}

p.submit input {
  font-size: 1.3em;
}

#help {
  display: none;
}

body.with-help {
  margin-right: 350px;
}

body.with-help #help {
  display: block;
  background: #F4EEBC;
  border: 1px solid #000;
  border-color: #CCC #333 #333 #CCC;
  width: 320px;
  position: absolute;
```

```
  top: 0;
  right: 0;
  margin: 8px 30px;
  padding: 10px;
  overflow: hidden;
}

#help p, #help h2 {
  width: 300px;
}

#help p#close_help {
  position: absolute;
  top: 0;
  right: 15px;
  width: auto;
}

#close_help a {
  color: black;
  text-decoration: none;
  font-weight: bold;
}

#loader {
  position: absolute;
  top: 10px;
  right: 10px;
}
```

Listing 9-6. *The application javascript file* (public/javascripts/application.js)

```
Event.addBehavior({
  'a[rel=help]:click' : function() {
    Help.openWith(this.href);
    return false;
  },
  '#close_help a:click' : function() {
    Help.close();
    return false;
  },
  '#header' : function() {
    Loader.initialize(this);
  }
});
```

```
Help = {
  openWith : function(url) {
    var urlParts = url.split('#');
    var path = urlParts[0], anchor = urlParts[1];

    this.request(url, function() {
      if ($(document.body).hasClassName('with-help') == false) this.open();

      if (anchor && (anchorEl = $(anchor))) {
        anchorEl.scrollTo();
        anchorEl.addClassName('highlighted');
      }
    });
  },
  open : function() {
    Help.fx.openHelp.custom(0, 320);
    Help.fx.slideBody.custom(30, 350);
  },
  close : function() {
    Help.fx.closeHelp.custom(320, 0);
    Help.fx.slideBody.custom(350, 30);
  },
  request : function(url, callback) {
    new Ajax.Updater('help', url, {
      method: 'get',
      onComplete: callback.bind(this)
    });
  }
};

Event.onReady(function() {
  Help.fx = {
    openHelp: new fx.Style('help', 'width', {
      onStart : function() {
        $(document.body).addClassName('with-help');
      }
    }),
    closeHelp: new fx.Style('help', 'width', {
      onComplete : function() {
        $(document.body).removeClassName('with-help');
      }
    }),
    slideBody: new fx.Style(document.body, 'margin-right')
  };
});
```

```
Loader = {
  initialize: function(parent) {
    this.loader = $img({ src: 'images/loader.gif', alt: 'Loading...', id:
'loader' });
    parent.appendChild(this.loader);
    this.hide();

    Ajax.Responders.register({
      onCreate: function() {
        Loader.show();
      },
      onComplete: function() {
        Loader.hide();
      }
    });
  },
  show: function() {
    this.loader.show();
  },
  hide: function() {
    this.loader.hide();
  }
};
```

Index

Find it faster at http://superindex.apress.com/

forums.apress.com

You Need the Companion eBook

Your purchase of this book entitles you to buy the companion PDF-version eBook for only $10. Take the weightless companion with you anywhere.

We believe this Apress title will prove so indispensable that you'll want to carry it with you everywhere, which is why we are offering the companion eBook (in PDF format) for $10 to customers who purchase this book now. Convenient and fully searchable, the PDF version of any content-rich, page-heavy Apress book makes a valuable addition to your programming library. You can easily find and copy code—or perform examples by quickly toggling between instructions and the application. Even simultaneously tackling a donut, diet soda, and complex code becomes simplified with hands-free eBooks!

Once you purchase your book, getting the $10 companion eBook is simple:

❶ Visit **www.apress.com/promo/tendollars/**.

❷ Complete a basic registration form to receive a randomly generated question about this title.

❸ Answer the question correctly in 60 seconds, and you will receive a promotional code to redeem for the $10.00 eBook.

2855 TELEGRAPH AVENUE | SUITE 600 | BERKELEY, CA 94705

Offer valid through 3/24/08.